DACOR BACON HOUSE

WILLIAM D. CALDERHEAD

DACOR BACON HOUSE FOUNDATION

WASHINGTON, D.C.

TO DACORIANS PAST, PRESENT, AND FUTURE

William D. Calderhead served for thirty-five years in the Foreign Service and has been an active member of DACOR and the DACOR Bacon House Foundation. A former member of the board of directors and chairman of the house committee, he currently serves as curator of the house.

Printed in the United States of America

5 4 3 2 1

Produced by Archetype Press, Inc., Washington, D.C.
Diane Maddex, Project Director
John Hovanec and Gretchen Smith Mui, Editors
Robert L. Wiser, Designer

Front cover: DACOR Bacon House
Back cover: The dining room on the second floor
Page 1: The north drawing room mirror and fireplace, painting by Lily Spandorf, circa 1950
Pages 2–3: Watercolor of DACOR Bacon House, painting by Pierre Landy, 1959
Right: The north drawing room, with a portrait of Abigail Smith Babcock, Virginia Bacon's great-great-great-aunt
Pages 6–7: The garden room, featuring a portrait of Virginia Bacon at age sixteen
Page 160: DACOR Bacon House, drawing by Babs Guillard, 1988

CONTENTS

PREFACE

Members of DACOR (Diplomatic and Consular Officers, Retired) have been privileged since 1986 to conduct their educational, cultural, charitable, and social endeavors in the historic setting of DACOR Bacon House. In the beginning, like most Dacorians, I was content to enjoy the grandeur and beauty of the great house without being aware either of its architectural evolution from its original 1824 design or of the background of the several families who had lived in it since it was built. Over the ensuing years, however, I heard and read many stories about the house and its owners. As my fascination grew, I was prompted to gather additional facts to flesh out and link together this information to produce a brief history. What follows is that history.

The south drawing room is dominated by an eighteenth-century tapestry. On the left is a portrait of John Murray, Virginia Bacon's paternal great-great-grandfather, who was the last royal governor-general of Virginia.

Listed in the National Register of Historic Places, DACOR Bacon House is a historically significant Federal-style home, an icon in Washington's inventory of early-nineteenth-century houses, and a landmark in America's heritage. For the first 160 years of its existence it was a private home, and the intertwined history of the house and the families who built, owned, adorned, enlarged, and modernized it is a fascinating tale.

This history is intended to enhance readers' enjoyment of their visits to DACOR Bacon House. For Dacorians, it should also generate a greater awareness of their responsibility in preserving for future generations not only the historic structure and grounds but also its treasure trove of antiques and Foreign Service memorabilia.

ACKNOWLEDGMENTS

The gallery is shown in 1988 as it appeared following the DACOR Bacon House Foundation's renovation and redecoration of 1985–86.

At every turn when writing this history of DACOR Bacon House, I was assisted and encouraged by many people. Especially important was the information I was able to gather from Virginia Murray Bacon's personal papers, now held by the Georgetown University Library. These papers provided a wealth of information about the house and Virginia Bacon's fifty-seven-year residence in it.

To Mary Thacher, librarian, the Stonington Historical Society of Stonington, Connecticut, I owe special thanks. For some time she has been researching the life of Virginia Bacon's maternal grandfather, Samuel Denison Babcock, and during visits to Washington and through correspondence she generously shared her material and family pictures with me.

I extend my thanks to Ambassador Lucius D. Battle and to Richard H. Howland for recounting their experiences in forming the DACOR Bacon House Foundation and conducting its affairs. My gratitude goes also to Dr. Josephine L. Murray, Virginia Bacon's niece, and Lawrence Kolp, Virginia Bacon's private secretary and curator for fourteen years, for sharing their recollections about the Murray and Bacon families.

Along the way, I benefited greatly from the assistance of staff members at the Library of Congress, the U.S. Supreme Court, the Supreme Court Historical Society, the Historical Society of Washington, D.C., the Historical Society of Maryland, the Office of the Governor of Maryland, the District of Columbia Recorder of Deeds, and the public libraries of both

the District of Columbia and Maryland. These professionals were always reliable in giving me valuable guidance and access to research material.

Greatly appreciated throughout this project was the unfailing cheerfulness and patience of my wife, Norma Jean, and DACOR staff members Carole Thomas and Cherie Whitney. Over many months they typed and retyped initial and revised drafts. Finally, my appreciation goes to DACOR's executive director, William W. Lehfeldt, who proffered helpful editorial guidance, questioned, culled, and suggested improvements. He also generously arranged for editing by Margery Boichel Thompson.

The assistance of these friends and colleagues contributed in important ways to the development of this history. I am deeply grateful to each of them.

The Battle-Torbert library houses Foreign Service memorabilia from around the world (above), the staircase features a wooden wainscot (opposite), and the dining room provides an elegant setting for formal entertainment (overleaf).

VIRGINIA MURRAY.

PROLOGUE

A LANDMARK KEEPSAKE

The Bacon mansion, about 1930, was surrounded mostly by private homes. Over the next three decades the area would grow to become a center for government and commercial offices. [DACOR Bacon House Foundation Collection]

PROXIMITY to the "President's House" was an important consideration in selecting a home site in the nation's capital in the early 1800s. It was mostly a matter of prestige and, to a lesser degree, of convenience that prompted the affluent and powerful to build fashionable trophy homes almost in the shadow of the presidential mansion. Few of these old showcase dwellings remain. But two blocks from the White House—at 1800 F Street, N.W.—perched in quiet splendor amid government and commercial neighbors stands one notable survivor: historic DACOR Bacon House.

DACOR Bacon House is one of the finest and best preserved early-nineteenth-century landmarks in Washington, D.C. As an architectural treasure, the house lends beauty and vitality to the city. As a microcosm of the capital city's social and cultural history, it reflects the lives of notable people and historic events.

Recounting the history of the house entails much more than bricks and mortar. It also involves the families who have owned and rented the house since it was built, a period of more than a century and a half, and the people who resided there as boarders. Between 1825 and 1980, the house was home to a U.S. marshal for the District of Columbia; two chief justices of the U.S. Supreme Court, several associate justices, and a clerk; a former two-term

governor of Maryland; a socially prominent Pittsburgh heiress and one-time English countess; a nationally recognized economist and original member of the Federal Reserve Board; a well-known international lawyer; a U.S. senator from Illinois; a U.S. representative from New York, and one of Washington's most endearing and enduring social leaders.[1] The story also concerns the building's transition in 1980 from a private home to the offices of the Bacon House Foundation, merged in 1985 into the DACOR Bacon House Foundation. Today, the historic edifice accommodates the headquarters and programs of the 2,300-member organization known as Diplomatic and Consular Officers, Retired, or, more familiarly, DACOR.

To enter DACOR Bacon House is to walk in the footsteps of a who's who of leaders of earlier times—men and women who helped chart our country's nation-building efforts, define its national interests, and conduct its relations with foreign governments. If the walls of the house could talk, they would recount conversations of the presidents, justices, governors, senators, representatives, diplomats, military leaders, international dignitaries, and leading social and cultural figures who graced the rooms at dinners and receptions, balls, and musicales. Political talk no doubt ran high about presidential candidates, congressional elections, foreign armed conflicts, treaties, annexation of territories, admission of new states to the Union, secession, and civil war. One can imagine heated discussions about President Lincoln's assassination and President Theodore Roosevelt's escapades in Cuba and Panama.

It would be fascinating, too, to eavesdrop on the members of Chief Justice Melville Weston Fuller's Supreme Court, which convened at the house on Saturdays from 1896 to 1910, as they deliberated the constitutionality of such matters as the Sherman Anti-Trust Act, legislation establishing a tax on personal income, and the "insular cases," which led to the formulation of a U.S. policy for colonial rule over territories outside the continental boundaries. Whispered bits of gossip about matchmaking, rivalries, and parties would no doubt titillate, as would banter about social customs, changing mores, travels, and families.

The last private owner of the house was Virginia Murray Bacon, the wife of Robert Low Bacon, who lived here until her death in 1980. A member of Old Guard society in both Washington, D.C., and New York City, she entertained often and in grand style and pursued her social rounds in a chauffeur-driven Rolls-Royce, the big old-fashioned kind with head-turning appeal.

The south drawing room is shown as it appeared in 1930. On the death of her mother in 1940, Virginia Bacon acquired a large collection of family portraits that sparked the redecoration of this and the adjoining entertainment rooms. [DACOR Bacon House Foundation Collection]

During the 1930s and 1940s, Virginia Bacon held a pivotal position in Washington society as one of the "three Bs." A trinity of good friends and patrons of the arts, each lived in luxury in an old and historically important home—Marie (Mrs. Truxtun) Beale in Decatur House on Lafayette Park, Mildred Barnes (Mrs. Robert Woods) Bliss in Dumbarton Oaks in Georgetown, and Virginia Bacon in her historic house at 1800 F Street. So dominant a force were they that anyone seeking acceptance into the city's social circles was advised to call on the "three Bs" before dropping cards at the White House. As the last survivor of the group, Virginia Bacon was sometimes called the last of Washington's grandes dames.[2]

Virginia Bacon's home was both elegant and grand. Although no one would ever call her whimsical, she sometimes exhibited a witty turn of mind in hosting some of her more fanciful parties. Perhaps she inherited her lighter side from her paternal great-great-grandfather, John Murray, fourth earl of Dunmore and the last royal governor-general of the colony of Virginia. Lord Dunmore indeed displayed a whimsical bent when, after fleeing the colonies and returning to Scotland at the onset of the American Revolution, he constructed on his estate in Stirlingshire, Scotland, just north of Glasgow, a limestone summerhouse he called the Pineapple. Much taken with the old southern custom of sailors spiking a pineapple on their gatepost to announce their return home, he transplanted the idea to Scotland and built a single-story, Gothic-winged structure with a tall, pineapple-topped tower. When traveling in Scotland, Virginia Bacon always visited the Dunmore estate and the pineapple summerhouse. On such occasions she no doubt enjoyed a good laugh at the expense of her famous ancestor, whose folly seemed to cast a spell of silliness on visitors, one of whom called the structure the "old fruit." The impression, visitors attested, was a happy one.[3]

DACOR Bacon House stands on land originally part of Prince George's County, Maryland. For most of the eighteenth century it was a tiny part of a large farm of several hundred acres that cut a swath through the heart of what is today downtown Washington. The original owner of the land was David Burnes, a Scottish immigrant; he and his descendants—his son, grandson, and great-granddaughter—in turn held, enlarged, and passed on these holdings until they encompassed more than six hundred acres.[4]

In 1791, as the federal city began to take shape, a portion of the Burneses' holdings was sold to the federal government for the construction of office buildings. Then, at the beginning of the nineteenth century, the three lots that today make up the DACOR Bacon House site were sold and resold to a succession of prominent citizens.

It was U.S. Marshal Tench Ringgold who bought the site and built the original house in 1824–25. That first house was an almost square, two-and-one-half-story structure erected on a full, above-ground English-style basement. The house we see today is obviously not the one completed in 1825. It has been significantly enlarged twice and thoroughly renovated several times. Yet, for all the changes, the last a $2 million, top-to-bottom restoration carried out in 1983–86, the house still retains much of its original scale, craftsmanship, and appeal. Outside and in, for viewers and users alike, it still evokes an early-nineteenth-century sense of time and place.

The stately four-story, twenty-four-room mansion and its adjoining carriage house, together with a half-acre garden and a bricked rear courtyard, occupy a quarter-block site in square 142 at the corner of 18th and

F Streets, N.W. Its next-door neighbor, the Organization of American States, occupies the remainder of the north side of the 1800 block of F Street. Backing up to the house's northern boundary, and occupying the remainder of square 142, is an office building with its entrance on G Street. Other nearby neighbors include the Old Executive Office Building, Winder Building, U.S. General Services Administration Building, World Bank, and George Washington University.

Today the mansion's spacious ceremonial and entertainment rooms, several with working fireplaces and antique candlelight chandeliers, provide settings of impressive charm and refinement. A bounty of antique continental and oriental furnishings, along with an eclectic mix of portraits, decorative arts, and Foreign Service memorabilia, imbues the house with elegance. The enclosed garden—a miniarboretum of shrubs, trees, and flowers—complements the interior entertainment facilities and contributes to the overall setting. The DACOR Bacon House Foundation, which owns the house, and the National Trust for Historic Preservation, which holds an easement for its "scenic open space and architectural facade," share the task of preserving this structure for future generations.[5]

If it is true that the era of entertaining in the grand manner has passed, then DACOR Bacon House stands as a gracious monument to those halcyon yet turbulent days. At every turn one can still sense Virginia Bacon's presence in the welcoming, enchanting feel of the house. As she once remarked, "It is a house that wants to be amused."[6] A gathering place since the young days of the Republic for the rich, the powerful, and the famous in their pursuit of intellectual hospitality, the house has clearly provided, and enjoyed, a full measure of amusement.

CHAPTER ONE

THE CAPITAL TAKES FORM

1721–1814

Washington, D.C., in the late 1700s was a series of farms and forested hills. This view looking east from Georgetown reveals how little development had occurred in the area. [Collection of the Historical Society of Washington, D.C.]

On July 16, 1790, meeting in New York City following the adoption of the U.S. Constitution in Philadelphia, the First Congress declared that the "Federal City," now named Washington, D.C., would become the nation's permanent capital in the fall of 1800. At the time, the future capital was little more than a series of thickly forested rolling hills divided into two dozen farms. The area between Jenkins Hill, today Capitol Hill, and the future president's mansion, at the other end of what would become Pennsylvania Avenue, was mostly swampy land laced with canals and drainage ditches. Yet, in this undeveloped ten-mile-square area, split by the Potomac River and formed by land ceded by Maryland and Virginia, a new capital was destined to emerge.[1]

To impose a sense of order on property boundaries and land ownership, President George Washington appointed a commission to divide the capital-to-be into streets and standard-size lots. To ensure that the federal government's interests would be protected, the commission was also authorized to purchase all properties necessary "to provide suitable buildings for the accommodation of Congress and the President and for public offices of the Government in time for their occupancy in 1800."[2]

Central to this effort was Pierre Charles L'Enfant, who had fought with General Washington in the Revolutionary War. It was to L'Enfant that

Washington turned in 1790 to prepare a master plan for the new city. Born in Paris and raised at the Palace of Versailles, L'Enfant envisaged a magnificent city along grand European lines. His plan, similar to one sketched by Thomas Jefferson, called for broad avenues, wide streets, and sweeping circles lined with ornate government buildings. It designated areas for residential sections of distinction and for public parks. It also projected a deep-water river port to foster industry, interstate commerce, and international trade.[3]

Early viewers of the plan greatly admired its sweep and grandeur. But some of the nation's leaders considered it unrealistic and expressed skepticism about the country's ability to finance it. Even his staunchest supporters, in and out of government, were irritated by L'Enfant's reluctance to simplify his plan. In February 1792, responding to growing opposition, President Washington discharged L'Enfant and in his place hired Andrew Ellicott, the surveyor who had first laid out the boundaries for the ten-mile-square "Territory of Columbia."

While generally retaining L'Enfant's basic concept for streets and hubs, Ellicott simplified the details, reduced the number of out-of-scale projects, and completed laying out standard-size lots. In November 1792, anxious to get on with the actual work, President Washington and Congress adopted the revised plan.[4] An engraving of Ellicott's finished 1792 survey, which he called "Out Lines of the City of Washington with the grand Avenues and principal Streets leading through the public appropriations," hangs in DACOR Bacon House today. The square in which DACOR Bacon House is located was identified on the plan as 142, a designation that has remained unchanged.

During the earliest years, the capital grew in an unstructured way. The few homes, boarding houses, and business places built before 1795 were scattered in haphazard fashion throughout the city. During the same period, only two government buildings were completed. Early visitors described the emerging capital as a city of broad avenues without houses, while nearby Georgetown was seen as a place of houses without streets. To encourage a sense of order and direction for future construction, a frustrated President Washington in 1796 directed that the executive departments of government be located in the vicinity of the White House. In the wake of that decision, the western reaches of the city quickly gained in both prestige and preeminence, and the area around the executive mansion became a choice neighborhood, where solidly built brick homes were

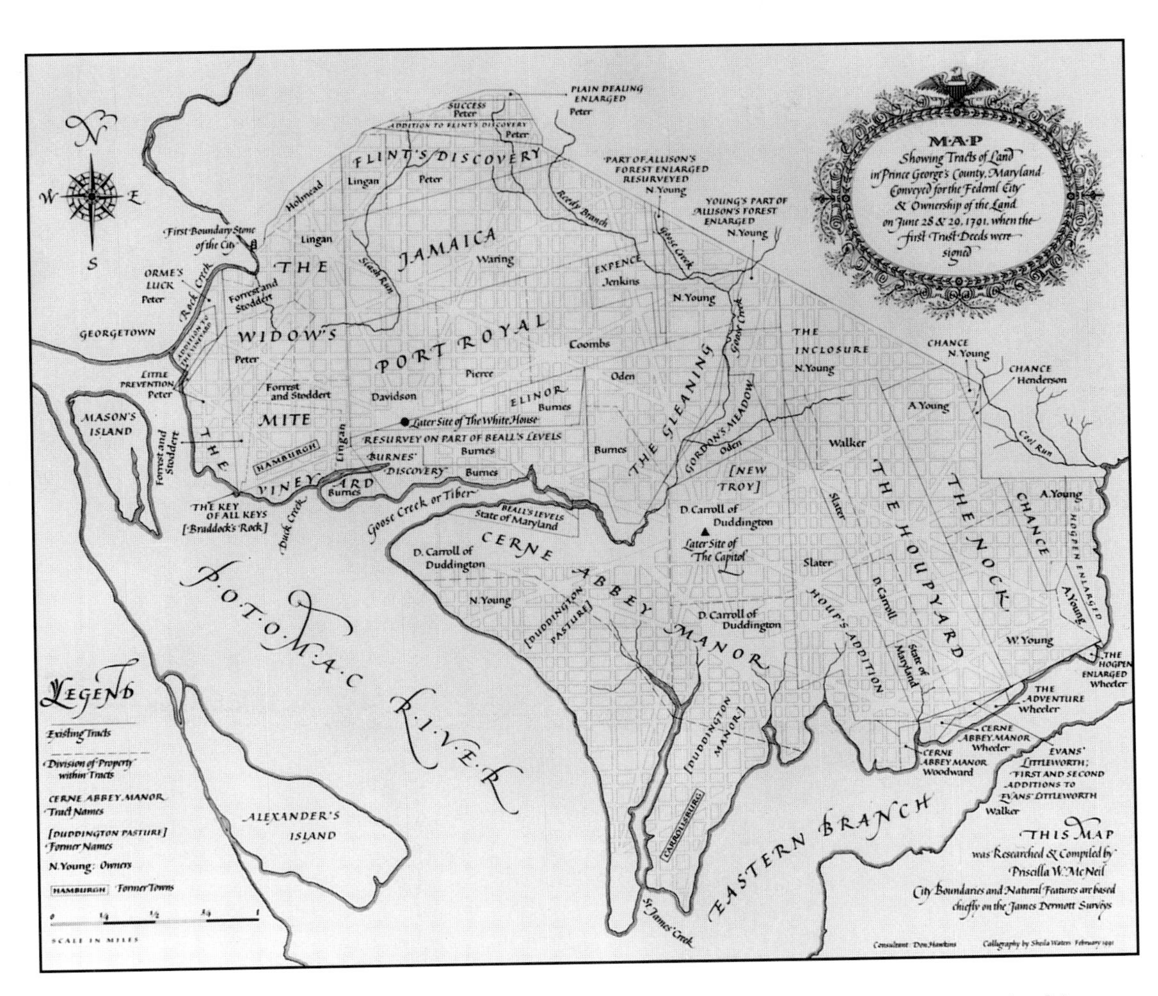

This map of the capital-to-be superimposes the planned streets of the new city over the early farm tracts and their proprietors. David Burnes's property is west of the present-day Capitol. [Collection of the Historical Society of Washington, D.C.]

mingled at random with federal department annexes.[5] It was in this area, a quarter of a century later, that DACOR Bacon House would be built in the Federal style so popular at the time and that today clearly evokes a sense of the early nineteenth century.

A U.S. Geological Survey map dated 1791, on file in the Library of Congress, shows that the present-day DACOR Bacon House property was at that time part of a farm tract owned by David Burnes II. His grandfather, David Burnes, after emigrating from Scotland in 1721, acquired the first of the family's real estate holdings by purchasing a section of land, originally identified as lying in Prince George's County, Maryland, that today would form part of downtown Washington. Over the years he expanded his holdings until they totalled 527 acres, embracing everything from H Street, N.W., on the north to Constitution Avenue, N.W., on the

David Burnes II's cottage (left), built about 1750, was captured in a watercolor by Henry Livingston Hillyer. When razed in 1894, it was the oldest extant building in the District of Columbia. [Collection of the Washington County Museum of Fine Arts, Hagerstown, Maryland]

The 1816 Van Ness mansion (opposite), whose southwest facade is shown, was the home of General John Peter Van Ness and Marcia Burnes Van Ness. Today the property is the site of the Pan-American Union Building. [Library of Congress]

south and from Third Street, N.W., westward to the Potomac River. Early records describe the land as sparsely wooded and mostly marsh, but on it Burnes successfully grew crops for personal use, barter, and export. Upon his death the farm passed to his son James, who expanded it to more than six hundred acres, and in 1772 to his grandson, David Burnes II, who fought as a lieutenant in the Revolutionary War.

As the owner of an important section of the land needed to create the core of the new capital, David Burnes II and other property owners were asked to convey to the United States in trust all the land they controlled within the boundaries of the new federal city. The government's plan, as proposed, was to pay nothing for the area set aside on L'Enfant's map for public buildings and streets. Of the remainder of Burnes's property, half would be purchased at a fixed per-lot price and half would remain under his control.

Finding the offered price inadequate and seeing the development of the new capital as a threat to his interests, Burnes refused to cooperate. Because of his unyielding stance, he became known among the commissioners as "the obstinate Mr. Burnes." Finally, on March 30, 1791, under

great pressure, including personal intervention by President Washington, Burnes agreed to sell the land that today forms a major segment of the Mall and the south half of the White House grounds. As stipulated, the government purchased half his holdings, and the commissioners allotted to him the remaining half, which included the lots occupied by DACOR Bacon House. In September 1791 the commissioners named the ten-mile square the "District of Columbia" and the capital-to-be "City of Washington."[6]

David Burnes II died intestate in 1800 (he is buried in Rock Creek Cemetery, where DACOR's memorial section is located), and his property, then valued at $1.5 million, passed to his teenage daughter, Marcia Brown Burnes. Taking advantage of the demand for property in the developing capital, her guardian, John Oakley, acting with court permission, began selling some of her property. Before doing so, however, he set aside for the use of Burnes's widow, Anne, and her two children a six-acre tract that fronted on 17th Street at Constitution Avenue. In 1802 Marcia married U.S. Representative John Peter Van Ness of New York, and in 1816 the now-General and Mrs. Van Ness built a lavish mansion on that site.

The mansion, designed by Benjamin Henry Latrobe, was said to be one of the grandest homes in the United States and was a favorite gathering place for the nation's leaders. General Van Ness was one of the three commissioners appointed by President James Madison to oversee the rebuilding of the public buildings burned by the British in 1814, and he twice served as mayor of Washington in the 1830s. He was also vice president (John Marshall was president) of the Washington National Monument Society, which sponsored the building of the Washington Monument as a memorial to "the father of our country." In the summer of 1832 a cholera epidemic swept the city and the nearby countryside, and Marcia Van Ness, leading a community effort to nurse the afflicted, contracted the disease and died. General Van Ness died in 1846. The Van Ness mansion, after years of neglect, was torn down in 1894.[7] (Today the site is occupied by the Pan-American Union Building.)

Among the lots sold by John Oakley on behalf of Marcia Burnes were the three lots on F Street now comprising the DACOR Bacon House property. The sale was carried out under a court decree (*Dorsey v. Burnes*) of April 24, 1802, which conveyed title to the property to William Hammond Dorsey. On the same date Anne Burnes conveyed to Dorsey her dower interest in the same property. Dorsey was a prominent member of the Georgetown community and of the committee of Georgetown leaders who received President John Adams on his arrival in the new capital in June 1800. A judge of the Orphan's Court of Washington County, Maryland, from 1801 to 1806, he had built a house on R Street in 1800 that, now enlarged and much changed, is known today as Dumbarton Oaks.

How Dorsey intended to use the F Street property is not clear. In any event, he retained it for only a brief period before selling it on December 14, 1803, to Colonel John Tayloe, who had built Octagon House at the corner of 18th Street and New York Avenue two years earlier. Then, in yet another double transaction, Dorsey repurchased the property from Tayloe on April 28, 1806, and resold it two months later to Jacob Wagner.[8]

Wagner was chief clerk of the Department of State from 1798 to 1807. He was also one of the owners of the Baltimore-based newspaper the *Federal Republican,* an organ of the Federalist Party. In 1812, after the United States declared war on England, this newspaper initiated a series of strong antiwar articles that succeeded in stirring violent partisan feelings against President Madison. Seeking revenge, an angry mob of the president's supporters gathered in Baltimore a few weeks after the series appeared, attacked the newspaper's offices, and destroyed them.

Undaunted and determined, Wagner quickly moved his printing presses from Baltimore to Georgetown, at the corner of 30th and M Streets, and continued his editorial barrage. Federalist friends, hearing about a new attack being planned by Madison's supporters, armed themselves and hastily assembled in Wagner's home, where the latest papers were being distributed. In the violent fighting that ensued, several people lost their lives. The Wagner house, scene of this second riot, fronted on the 1800 block of G Street, N.W.; its garden abutted the present-day DACOR Bacon House property on F Street.[9]

From 1790, when Congress voted to establish the federal city, to 1815, when the capital was recovering from the destruction wrought in 1814 by the British invaders—a period of twenty-five years—a small city emerged from what had been forested hills dotted with a few dozen scattered houses. By 1800, 109 buildings of brick and 263 of wood had been built, and the population numbered 615 families with 3,210 members. By 1803 the population had grown to 4,352 people, and the census of 1807 counted 6,552 people. Increasing by approximately five hundred persons a year, the city took on the appearance and pulse of a prosperous and growing government center.

During this period ditches were dug to drain off the swampy areas and make them usable. Footpaths became common, and one six-foot-wide sidewalk, partially topped with stone chips from the Capitol, extended from the Capitol to Rock Creek. Sturdy bridges were built over Tiber and Rock Creeks. Hotels and boarding houses sprang up, and the United States Theater, the city's first place of entertainment, opened in the Great Hotel. Some of the credit for bringing order out of the original chaos must go to Benjamin Henry Latrobe, who designed the Capitol. Both as city surveyor and as superintendent of buildings, he established standards of excellence that others were quite willing to follow.

Some of the country's best educated, wealthiest, and most dedicated citizens now lived in the city of Washington, so it is not surprising that a society of charm and elegance emerged. As the city grew, new homes were built in every section, and the number and variety of stores and businesses needed to serve the expanding population inevitably increased. The few attempts to mount heavy industry failed, however. With government machinery as its base, the capital would presumably enjoy uninterrupted growth while maintaining its unique nonindustrialized character.[10]

CHAPTER TWO

PROPERTY OF A PRESIDENT'S SECRETARY

1815–1824

On May 3, 1815, Jacob Wagner sold the F Street property to Tobias Lear V. The exact date the Lear family emigrated from England to America is not known, but the marriage of the first Tobias Lear, to Elizabeth Sherburne Langdon, was recorded in Portsmouth, New Hampshire, on April 11, 1667. The couple had two daughters and a son, Tobias Lear II, father of Tobias III, who married Elizabeth Hall. Their son, Tobias IV, married Mary Stillson, and from this marriage came Tobias Lear V in 1762. It was this last Lear, followed by his widow and son, who owned the present DACOR Bacon House property from 1815 to 1824.[1]

Tobias Lear, private secretary to George Washington, owned the property at 1801 F Street from 1815 to 1816. His widow and son held it until 1824, when they sold the land to Tench Ringgold. Lear's portrait was painted in 1798 by James Sharples. [Frick Art Reference Library]

Tobias Lear V is best remembered as the young New Hampshire gentleman and Harvard graduate who was hired by George Washington as "preceptor to my children and clerk and private secretary to me."[2] In 1785 Washington, seeking help in finding an assistant, had turned to his old army comrade Benjamin Lincoln, who had served as secretary of war in 1781. Lincoln's son commended Lear to his father, who in turn suggested him to Washington. Impressed with the young man's qualifications, Washington hired Lear on May 29, 1786, at an annual salary of $200.

In the letters effecting the deal, Washington said, "He will sit at my table, will live as I live, will mix with the company who resort to the house,

and will be treated with every respect and civility and proper attention."[3] Lear, living as one of the family at Mount Vernon, met and dined with all those who came to exchange views with Washington on the task of building a new nation. When Washington was inaugurated as the first president of the United States on April 30, 1789, Lear merely added the duties of private secretary to the president to his earlier responsibilities and continued to live with the first family in the presidential mansions in both New York City and Philadelphia.

Mystery surrounds both the artist and the subject of this painting. It is believed to be a portrait of George Washington painted by Robert Fulton, although no evidence can confirm either identity. [C. E. Anderson, DACOR Bacon House Foundation Collection]

The first presidential mansion in New York, at 1 Cherry Street (no longer extant), was rented by the government from one of the American ancestors of Virginia Bacon. A photograph of a circa 1790 lithograph of the house is on display in the garden room of DACOR Bacon House. A footnote reads: "The first Presidential Mansion, owned by Walter Franklin. It was selected by the Government as the most fitting abode for George Washington when he entered office in 1789. His gracious letter to the family upon vacating the house became the possession of Anthony Franklin, the great-grandfather of Fannie Morris Babcock [Virginia Bacon's mother]." In March 1793 Tobias Lear elected to leave his position with President Washington and, with Washington's support, embarked on a business career in the new capital-to-be as a land speculator and importer-exporter. Despite the formal separation, Lear remained close to Washington, often visiting Mount Vernon. In 1798 he became Washington's chief aide, with the rank of colonel, and was holding his hand when Washington died in 1799.[4]

Today the John F. Kennedy Center for the Performing Arts and Rock Creek Parkway sit atop the riverfront lots where Lear's wharf was located and from where he conducted the affairs of T. Lear and Company.[5] For a few years he was also president of the Potomack Canal Company, which George Washington had cofounded and originally headed and which

The first presidential mansion was located at 1 Cherry Street in New York City. The government rented the house from Walter Franklin, maternal great-great-great-grand-father of Virginia Bacon. [C. E. Anderson, DACOR Bacon House Foundation Collection]

unsuccessfully sought to create a navigable waterway from the Potomac River in Georgetown to the Ohio River.[6]

In 1801, when Lear's business ventures waned, he turned to his old friend Thomas Jefferson, who had recently been inaugurated the third president of the United States. Through Jefferson, a close friend for many years, Lear gained an appointment as American consul in Santo Domingo, now the Dominican Republic. At the time Santo Domingo was considered a French possession, although an independence movement headed by Toussaint L'Ouverture was under way and making steady progress. Whether Lear sympathized with the movement is unclear, but when Napoleon sent General Charles Victor Emmanuel LeClerc with twenty thousand troops to take possession of the island in preparation for extending the French empire to present-day Louisiana, the general ordered the American consul to leave. Unsuccessfully protesting his expulsion, Lear reluctantly returned to the United States with his consular endeavors unfinished and his dream of a flourishing import-export business with the Caribbean islands unrealized.[7]

Lear was hardly settled again in Washington when President Jefferson, with the strong support of Secretary of State James Madison, named him consul general in Algiers, in which role he was charged with overseeing American interests with the various rulers along the Barbary Coast. Between 1803 and 1805, supported on occasion by the presence of U.S. naval forces, he successfully negotiated the Treaty of Tripoli with the ruling bey, Yusuf Bashaw. The treaty ended Tripoli's practice of exacting financial tribute from American vessels intercepted in Mediterranean waters. Lear resolved a similar shipping problem with neighboring Morocco, negotiating with the emperor of Morocco a clarification of the existing 1787 treaty of commerce and friendship between their two countries. He also succeeded in fostering peace with the dey of Algiers, Achmed Pasha, and in negotiating with the bey of Tunis, Hamouda Bashaw, to markedly improve relations with Tunisia.

By 1810, seven years into his consular assignment, Lear had tired of Algeria, and the Algerians had grown weary of him. Relations with the ruling dey were at a low point, the work bored him, and the social life had grown tedious. He was also appalled at the widespread violence and bloodshed that characterized life throughout the region. And both he and his wife, Frances, known as Fanny (his third wife), missed their nineteen-year-old son, Lincoln, whom they had not seen for eight years. As the months passed and Lear's appeals to return home went unheeded, his frustration grew. Perhaps reflecting his growing impatience in his reporting, Consul General Lear informed Secretary of State James Monroe in January 1811 that he was under intense pressure from the dey of Algiers to produce the United States's "annuity vessel." This periodic tribute consisted of a shipload of marine stores for the use of the dey's navy, and a list of the desired supplies had been sent months earlier to Washington for action.[8]

Time passed slowly, and Lear had no response. Finally, to his great relief, the American vessel *Alleghany* arrived in Algiers on July 17, 1812. A delighted dey watched the unloading get under way. He became furious, however, when he learned that he would not be receiving all of the requested stores, especially not the gunpowder. He was further insulted when he learned that the ship's manifest listed a large consignment of coffee for the emperor of Morocco but none for him. Now thoroughly indignant, the dey ordered the unloading to cease and informed Lear that he was expelled and must depart within three days. Before he would be permitted to leave, however, he was told to pay 21,000 sequins to the regency; if he failed to do so he was to be sent to prison in chains.[9]

Lear was understandably irritated by this irrational action and, had he been allowed to have an audience with the dey, would no doubt have lodged a polite protest and might even have hinted that some suitable retaliation by the American government could be expected. Whatever his mood, his actions were no doubt tempered by recalling that just three months earlier in March the Danish consul had been sent to prison in chains and made to labor as a slave for failing to pay the biennial present, even though it was not due for two more months. The imprisoned consul was eventually released through the intervention of the entire consular corps. Lear must also have recalled that in April the dey, for some perceived slight, had ordered the beheading of David Coen Bacri, the chief of the Hebrew nation in Algeria, and Ben Dacam, chief of the Hebrew nation in Algiers. Lacking any U.S. military presence to support him in negotiating the matter, Lear wisely chose the safe course, borrowed the money, and paid the required sum to the regency. Now free, but obliged to depart, Lear, his wife, and their son, who had just arrived in Algiers on July 15, boarded the *Alleghany* on July 25, 1812, and set sail for home.[10]

Lear was ecstatic to be homeward bound, but his happiness soon crumbled. With a long ocean voyage lying ahead, the ship's captain, of necessity, put into Gibraltar on July 28 to take on needed supplies. Making the most of the stopover, Lear visited his American counterpart, British officials, and various foreign consular representatives. Not surprisingly, everyone was friendly, for the news had not yet reached Gibraltar that the United States had declared war on Great Britain. Lear was also unaware of this state of affairs. When word of Madison's war against England, declared by Congress on June 18, 1812, reached Gibraltar, the port commander, Commodore Charles Penrose, immediately impounded the *Alleghany* and imprisoned the crew. Although Lear's diplomatic status enabled him to avoid formal internment, the absence of an American vessel to continue his journey in effect made him a prisoner of war as well.[11]

This situation continued for several months until Lear was informed in November that the cargo and equipment aboard all captured American vessels would be sold. In protesting this action he took the occasion to inform the commodore that, since the fate of the American vessels seemed to have been determined, there was no further reason for him to remain in Gibraltar to protect American shipping interests. In the circumstances, if permitted, he would proceed to Spain as soon as possible. As anxious to be rid of Lear as Lear was to depart, Commodore Penrose graciously provided passage aboard the British ship *Fanny*, which sailed on December 1 and deposited the Lear family in Cadiz on December 3.[12]

In Cadiz, Lear made the most of his freedom, calling on both Spanish officials and various foreign consular and diplomatic representatives. He also attended a ball given by the grandees of Spain in honor of Lord Wellington, who was visiting at the time. Always one to enjoy traveling about the countryside, he visited schools, a winery, and other points of interest, all the while writing more reports. Finally, on February 27, 1813, hearing through the captain of a visiting American vessel that the president thought it "proper that I should return to the United States," Lear, Fanny, and Lincoln boarded the American ship *Halcyon* and sailed for home. They arrived in New York on April 9, 1813, and in the nation's capital three weeks later, on April 29.[13]

Although weary from his travels, Lear immediately set about calling on President Madison and Secretary Monroe, as well as on various old friends. Among these were William Thornton, the first architect of the capitol, and Tristram Dalton, an old business partner. With these obligations out of the way and personal finances not a problem, the Lears enjoyed several weeks of leisure in Washington before traveling to New England. In Portsmouth, New Hampshire, his birthplace, Lear visited his mother and sister. In Portland, Maine, Bowdoin College conferred upon him an honorary master's degree. Wherever he went he was warmly received and routinely honored. He enjoyed the limelight.

With the onset of fall, however, the Lears returned to Washington, where they continued their carefree lifestyle during the early months of 1814. This tranquillity was briefly broken in June, when President Madison drafted him to negotiate with British authorities an exchange of the prisoners taken by both sides in fighting that had occurred near Plattsburgh, New York. Four weeks later, with the negotiations successfully concluded, Lear returned to Washington and accepted Madison's offer of the post of accountant in the War Department, roughly equivalent to comptroller.[14]

Just before accepting the position, Lear had dismissed as highly improbable a British attack on the capital. He had barely sat down at his desk when the British troops stormed Washington, sacked government offices, and burned many public buildings, including the White House. Ironically, in 1793 in his *Observations on the River Potomack, the Country*

Adjacent, and the City of Washington, Lear had written that "not a river in America is capable of being rendered more secure of an attack by water than the Potomack."[15] He also opined that the various projected government buildings, because they were to be built of white stone, would be indestructible. The five thousand invading British soldiers, led by Major General Robert Ross, proved him wrong on both points. In the aftermath of that debacle, Lear was offered, but did not accept, an appointment to the three-member presidential commission charged with overseeing the reconstruction of the destroyed public buildings.[16]

Tragically, and without explanation or apparent reason, Lear committed suicide on October 11, 1816, in what is now the garden of the DACOR Bacon House. He is buried in Oak Hill Cemetery in Georgetown. His wife, Fanny, who, like his second wife, was a niece of Martha Washington, held the property with her son, Benjamin, until February 28, 1824, when they sold it to Tench Ringgold. At that time the property was appraised at $800.[17]

CHAPTER THREE

MARSHALL AND THE JUSTICES MOVE IN

1824–1835

TENCH RINGGOLD was descended from Thomas Ringgold (1610–72), a Royalist who came to America from England in 1650 to escape the tyranny of Cromwell. His arrival marked the beginning of a family line that through succeeding generations produced leaders in the clergy, law, military, medicine, and commerce, as well as in state and national government. There were four more Thomas Ringgolds, including Thomas IV, a member of the House of Burgesses of Maryland, who coauthored a series of resolutions, focusing on the constitutional rights and privileges of freemen of the colonies, that were forerunners of the Bill of Rights. His son, Thomas Ringgold V, fathered another Thomas but also produced Tench Ringgold, his youngest son. The family of Thomas Ringgold V, including Tench, was raised in the Ringgold mansion, today called the Hynson-Ringgold House, in Chestertown, Maryland.[1] (The house is listed in the National Register of Historic Places and has served since 1946 as the president's house of Washington College.)

When Tench Ringgold bought the F Street property from the Lears in 1824, he was U.S. marshal for the District of Columbia, a post to which he had been appointed by President James Monroe. He retained the position through the administration of John Quincy Adams, serving until 1831, when newly elected President Andrew Jackson declined to reappoint

DACOR Bacon House, when built in 1824–25 by Tench Ringgold, was a two-and-one-half-story Federal-style structure on a full English (above ground) basement. This conceptual drawing by Zane Carter and Katherine J. McGwier shows how the original structure may have appeared. [DACOR Bacon House Foundation Collection]

F ST
18TH

him. In earlier years Ringgold, described as an obese and prosaic gentleman, had been the secretary of a Georgetown savings and loan association and had owned a leather tannery, rope factory, and sugar refinery.[2]

When the British burned Washington in 1814, Ringgold was with President Madison. They fled the capital together at the last minute, along with Secretary of War John Armstrong, Secretary of State Monroe, and Charles Carroll of Baltimore. After the British withdrew, President Madison appointed Ringgold to the three-member presidential commission in charge of repairing public structures.[3]

Ringgold's wife was the former Mary Christian Lee, the daughter of Thomas Sim Lee (1745–1819), who was the second and seventh governor of the state of Maryland. A Marylander by birth, Governor Lee was a close friend of George Washington and a member of the same family that gave us Henry "Light Horse Harry" Lee, the man who described George Washington as "first in war, first in peace, and first in the hearts of his countrymen."[4] General Robert E. Lee, commander of the Confederate forces during the Civil War, was also a member of this distinguished family, as was Blair Lee, a U.S. senator from Maryland in 1914–17.

Tench Ringgold's first house was built in 1812 at the corner of 25th and L Streets, N.W. The house was converted into the Columbia Hospital for Women and is the site of the present-day hospital. [Collection of the Historical Society of Washington, D.C.]

The house that Tench Ringgold built at 1801 F Street in 1824–25 was actually his second house in Washington. The first, constructed in 1812, was a large Federal-style house at 25th and L Streets, N.W. After moving to F Street, Ringgold rented his former residence to various notable personages, including, before the Civil War, two British ministers to the United States, Sir Charles Bagot and Sir Frederick W. A. Bruce. In 1872 Congress provided funds to purchase the property as a permanent site for the Columbia Hospital for Women, although the house survived until 1914, when it was razed to make way for the present main hospital building.[5]

Ringgold was able to build his F Street house only by borrowing $6,000 from his daughter, Sarah, the wife of John M. Thomas, and most likely using slaves, either his own or those belonging to neighbors or traders. (In the early nineteenth century, when Washington, D.C., was a major slave-trading center, both untrained laborers and skilled carpenters, bricklayers, and stonecutters were drawn from the city's black population, then 25 percent of the total population.) The original structure, a Federal-style home of Flemish bond brick, was forty-five feet by forty-seven feet and contained seven thousand square feet of space. The site consisted of three lots in square 142, with a 103-foot frontage on 18th Street and a 131.25-foot frontage on F Street. The two-and-one-half-story house had a double-gabled roof and was built on a full, above-ground English-style basement. Outside, a wrought-iron stair led directly from the sidewalk to a suite of entertainment rooms on the second floor, an arrangement obviously inspired by the *piano nobile* concept of eighteenth-century French architecture.[6]

Like many of his neighbors, Ringgold probably selected the Federal style of architecture because it was thought to symbolize the ideals of the new Republic and to be an expression of social order and purpose. Its exterior beauty derived from a fluid blending of red brick, red stone, wrought iron, and wood, while the quality of its details firmly established its architectural integrity and pedigree. Offering grace, dignity, and clarity of layout, the house included extraordinary entertainment space and previously unknown standards of convenience and comfort. Its entire service functions were under the main floor, out of sight and out of hearing.

The plan of Ringgold's house is said to be a mirror image of the original Blair House, located across Pennsylvania Avenue from the White House, which today, enlarged and greatly changed, serves as the president's guest house. Some historians speculate that Benjamin Henry Latrobe may have designed both houses. Because drawings for DACOR Bacon House are missing, as are those for some of Latrobe's most important works, it is possible, if unlikely, that he was the architect, as he moved to New Orleans in 1817 and died there four years before the house was built. It can be said that DACOR Bacon House fully meets Latrobe's criterion that a home should be "an elegant place of planned convenience and functionality for the family, as well as for carrying out impressive entertainments."[7]

John Marshall, chief justice of the Supreme Court from 1801 to 1835, boarded at 1801 F Street, N.W., from 1831 to 1832 and began a tradition that linked the Supreme Court to the house. His portrait is by Otto Schneider. [C. E. Anderson, DACOR Bacon House Foundation Collection]

Adjacent to the main house and along the north property line, Ringgold constructed two outbuildings. The smaller of the two, possibly a storage shed and probably of wood, was located in the northwest corner of the garden. A larger building, centered at the back of the house and easily accessible from 18th Street, was doubtless a carriage house. Both structures existed until the 1860s.

On March 4, 1825, at about the time their F Street house was nearing completion, the Ringgolds attended the swearing-in ceremony for John Quincy Adams, the sixth president of the United States. That evening they were guests at the Inaugural Ball, held at Caruso's Saloon on 11th Street and Pennsylvania Avenue, N.W. A year later, as Ringgold mourned the death of his wife, he also mourned the passing of two old friends, the former presidents Thomas Jefferson and John Adams. Both died on July 4, 1826, as the fiftieth anniversary of the United States's independence was being observed by the ten million citizens of the country's twenty-four states.

In keeping with the custom of the times, Ringgold offered board and lodging at 1801 F Street to government officials who came to Washington periodically to conduct the nation's business. Former President James Monroe and his wife stayed with Ringgold while passing through Washington in 1829 and in the winter of 1830. Over the years, Ringgold provided temporary lodging for many members of the Supreme Court. In 1831 and 1832 Chief Justice John Marshall and Associate Justice Joseph Story boarded at 1801 F Street. Congressional directories of the period

Joseph Story, associate justice of the Supreme Court from 1811 to 1845, boarded at the house from 1831 to 1832 during the same time John Marshall resided there. His portrait is by George P. A. Healey. [Collection of the Supreme Court of the United States]

show that Associate Justices William Johnson, Gabriel Duval, Smith Thompson, John McLean, and Henry Baldwin also boarded with Ringgold from time to time.[8]

Two bronze plaques mounted on the F Street facade of the house attest to the residency of John Marshall. The first plaque, installed in 1930 by the District of Columbia Daughters of the American Revolution, simply notes that Marshall "here lived for a time" and acknowledges Tench Ringgold as the man "who built and occupied" the mansion. The second plaque, erected in the 1930s under the auspices of the Columbia Historical Society and the Bar Association of the District of Columbia, identifies 1801 F Street as "the residence of Chief Justice John Marshall, Chief Justice Melville Fuller and Associate Justice Joseph Story."

Justice Story noted in early letters to his wife that he and Marshall kept "bachelor hall at the house in the most frank and unaffected intimacy. . . . Our social hours, when undisturbed with labors of the law, are passed in gay and frank conversation. We moot every question as we proceed, and by familiar conference at our lodgings often come to a very quick and, I trust, a very accurate opinion in a few hours. It is certainly true that the judges here live with perfect harmony and as agreeably as absence from friends and families could make our residence."[9]

On another occasion Justice Story wrote that "two of the Justices are widowers and are, of course, objects of considerable attraction among the ladies of the city. We have fine sport at their expense, and amuse our leisure with some touches of matchmaking. We have already ensnared one of the judges and he is now (at the age of forty-seven) violently affected with tender passion."[10]

Also credited to Justice Story is a tale that is still told at the Supreme Court. On rainy days the justices would often enliven their conferences with wine. Occasionally, Marshall might say: "Brother Story, step to the window and see if it doesn't look like rain." If Story reported the sun was shining Marshall would order wine anyway, saying, "All the better, for our jurisdiction extends over so vast a territory that the doctrine of chances makes it certain that it must be raining somewhere!"[11]

Before serving as chief justice from 1801 to 1835, John Marshall distinguished himself as an officer of the American forces during the Revolutionary War, U.S. envoy to France, secretary of war, and secretary of state. Students of the Supreme Court agree that the compelling force of Marshall's logic brought prestige to the court. His far-sighted opinions, inspiring the law to this day, helped mold the nation by upholding the powers of the union against claims for states' rights.[12]

Edward Douglass White Jr. was chief justice of the Supreme Court from 1910–21. White was the grandson of Tench Ringgold, who built the house in 1824–25. [Collection of the Supreme Court of the United States]

Associate Justice Story sat on the court from 1811 to 1845. His opinions in admiralty cases during the War of 1812 became models of international law; and it was he who in 1818 wrote the opinion that established the Supreme Court's right to judicial review of state court decisions. In 1837, upholding the broad view of the Constitution, he successfully argued that Congress had the exclusive right to regulate state and foreign commerce. His writings, such as his 1833 *Commentaries on the Constitution of the United States*, and his many court opinions still constitute important pillars of our judicial system.[13]

Tench Ringgold and his wife contributed directly as well as indirectly to the history of the U.S. Supreme Court. One of their five children, their second daughter, Catherine Sidney Lee Ringgold, married Edward Douglass White. An ardent member of the Whig Party, White was elected three times to the U.S. House of Representatives from St. Martin's Parish, Louisiana, serving from 1829 to 1834. During this period in Washington he met and married Catherine. In 1834 he resigned his congressional seat to become the seventh governor of Louisiana; but after completing his four-year term, 1835–39, he returned to Congress to represent his old district once again. In 1843 after he served two terms, the Whites returned to Louisiana, where in 1845 their fifth child, Edward Douglass White Jr., was born.

Like his father, Edward White Jr. became a lawyer. In 1874 he was elected to the Louisiana Senate and was later appointed associate justice of the Louisiana Supreme Court. Running as a Democrat in the national elections of 1890, he won a seat in the U.S. Senate. But four years into his six-year term he was nominated by President Grover Cleveland to fill the vacancy on the U.S. Supreme Court created by the death of Samuel Blatchford. Quickly confirmed by his Senate colleagues, he served as an associate justice until 1910, when President William Howard Taft elevated him to chief justice of the United States, an office he held until his death on May 19, 1921.[14]

Having served as U.S. marshal for the District of Columbia under Presidents James Monroe and John Quincy Adams, Ringgold had been gratified to receive indirect assurances from Monroe that he would continue to serve under President Andrew Jackson. When he was instead replaced a few weeks later by a Jackson ally, Henry Ashton, Ringgold was deeply shocked. Adams, in a diary entry dated February 16, 1831, relates the circumstances thus: "When [former president] Monroe was here last winter he dined with President Jackson, who treated him with affectionate respect and kindness; and on taking leave of him Mr. Monroe said to him that he might never see him again; that he would venture to ask him only one favor, and that was to recommend Marshal Ringgold to his kindness; and then he spoke with much feeling of the causes of his own attachment to Ringgold; upon which Jackson took Monroe's hand, pressed it between both his own, and said, 'Say not one word more, Mr. Monroe,' which Monroe took for an inviolable promise that Ringgold would be continued in place."[15]

On hearing of his dismissal, Ringgold sought to influence matters in his favor by presenting to President Jackson a petition, signed by eighteen hundred of the District's most prominent citizens, urging that he be retained in office. But, as Adams further noted in his diary, these solicitations "had not the weight of a feather" and had "gone in one ear and out the other."[16] Furthermore, although Ringgold had accompanied Jackson when he walked to the Capitol to be sworn in as the seventh president of the United States, Old Hickory, it seems, attached little importance to that act of friendship.

As noted earlier, Tench Ringgold had been raised in the house now known as the Hynson-Ringgold House in Chestertown, Maryland. That house, Elizabeth Duvall relates in her book, *Three Centuries of American Life,* was built circa 1745 by Dr. William Murray, who held it until 1767, when he sold it to Thomas Ringgold IV.[17] By an interesting coincidence, Dr. William Murray and Virginia Murray Bacon of DACOR Bacon House are both members of the same Scottish family. *Debrett's Peerage and Baronetage* reveals that Dr. William Murray springs from the house of Atholl, one of whose members was created the earl of Dunmore in 1686. Virginia Bacon's family is a branch of this same house of Atholl, and she is a direct-line descendant of the earls of Dunmore, the fourth of whom, John Murray, was her paternal great-great-grandfather.[18] Although they appeared on the American scene 167 years apart, Dr. William Murray and Virginia Murray Bacon share the distinction, respectively, of creating and preserving two important landmarks.

The various members of the Ringgold family, scattered throughout the eastern seaboard and the country, have distinguished themselves in many ways. When the first Thomas Ringgold arrived in America in 1650 he bought a thousand acres of Kent Island, Maryland, and doubled his holdings in 1659 through a patent granted him by Lord Baltimore. The buildings on these lands were passed down to succeeding generations, each of which enlarged their estates, sometimes through marriage, until by the early 1800s General Samuel Ringgold owned seventeen thousand acres. Each generation had also exhibited a creative entrepreneurial spirit that sparked a variety of profitable ventures. These included ship building; coastal and international trade; rope and soap factories; grain, wool, and sugar mills; and other light manufacturing. Several Ringgolds also engaged in the slave trade until 1783, when it was abolished in Maryland.[19]

Their wealth was also used to promote the public good. Thomas Ringgold IV, together with other contributors, provided the funds that enabled Charles Willson Peale, head of the Free School of Chestertown, to go to London to study painting. Thomas IV also gave generously to the school itself, which eventually became Washington College. Thomas V, prosperous, highly respected, and characterized by some as the most brilliant and experienced statesman in the colony of Maryland, is credited with drafting Maryland's constitution and shaping its republican form of government. His Chestertown home was a popular stopover for friends, among them George Washington and Benjamin Franklin, both of whom stayed there when passing through the area.[20]

U.S. Army General Samuel Ringgold, brother of Thomas VI, built Fountain Rock, a palatial home near Hagerstown, Maryland, said to be the grandest mansion in Maryland. There he entertained in lavish style such luminaries as Henry Clay, James Madison, and James Monroe. In 1792 General Ringgold married Anna Maria Cadwalader, daughter of

John Cadwalader, who had been George Washington's military aide. They had eleven children. After Anna Maria's death at age thirty-five, Samuel married Marie Antoinette Hay, daughter of George Hay and Elizabeth Monroe Hay, President Monroe's eldest daughter. The wedding ceremony was performed in the White House, where the Hays lived on with the Monroes for a considerable time after the wedding. Of the five children of this second marriage, a daughter, Virginia, later married John Ross Key and became the mother of Francis Scott Key. A son, Cadwalader Ringgold, became a U.S. naval officer and rose to the rank of rear admiral. He fought against the West Indian pirates and headed several surveying expeditions to the North Pacific, China Seas, Antarctic, and West Coast of America. Another son, Major Samuel Ringgold, graduated from West Point and fought in the Mexican War.[21]

Other family members also achieved a measure of fame. One was an American consul in Peru, one a published poet, one the mayor of Baltimore in 1887, and more than one served in Congress. Richard Williamson Ringgold was president of Washington College from 1832 to 1853, and the Ringgolds donated the third and fourth buildings, now known as East and West Halls, to be constructed on the campus.[22] Even today, various Ringgold descendants are Maryland residents, and some descendants of the Ringgold slaves probably still live on Maryland's Eastern Shore. A large and distinguished family, the Ringgolds' genealogical history is set forth on a superb chart held by the Maryland Historical Society in Baltimore.

As for Tench Ringgold, the loss of his U.S. marshal's position in 1831 stripped him of his political power and influence and marked the beginning of a period of economic hardship. As a consequence he soon defaulted on the $6,000 loan from his daughter, Sarah. In those difficult circumstances he urged Sarah and her husband, John M. Thomas, to initiate foreclosure proceedings by entering a "bill of complaint" in the District Court of the District of Columbia, "praying that Tench Ringgold be made defendant" for his failure to pay his debts. On May 27, 1833, the court decreed the sale of the F Street property with title vested in John Thomas. That fall, Tench abandoned his F Street house and moved his family out of Washington. Two years later, on April 12, 1835, Thomas sold the property to Samuel Sprigg, thus beginning the Sprigg-Carroll family's sixty-year stewardship of the property.[23]

CHAPTER FOUR

RAISING THE ROOF

1835–1895

Samuel Sprigg, painted by Charles Willson Peale, was governor of Maryland from 1819 to 1822 and owner of the house from 1835 to 1855. He was the father of Sarah Sprigg Carroll, who resided in the house from 1836 to 1895. [Courtesy Maryland State Archives]

SAMUEL SPRIGG, whose birth is not officially recorded, is believed to have been born about 1783, probably in Washington County, Maryland. The uncertainty of his date and place of birth aside, he is known to be a descendant of Thomas Sprigg, who emigrated from England to America in 1655. From that first Thomas Sprigg there is an unbroken line of eldest sons named Thomas that runs through four generations to Thomas Sprigg IV. Henrich E. Buchholz, in his book *Governors of Maryland,* notwithstanding some controversy, asserts in a convincing way that Samuel was the son of Thomas IV's brother, Joseph Sprigg, and Joseph's second wife, Margaret Weems Sprigg.

Little is known about Joseph Sprigg. His only documented achievement is his appointment as one of the original seven commissioners of Washington County, Maryland, following its creation on September 6, 1776. That appointment suggests that he must have been an important landowner and a recognized leader in the community. Following Joseph's death in 1800 his son, Samuel, then about sixteen years of age, was adopted by his uncle, Osborne Sprigg, and taken to live at the latter's estate in Prince George's County, Maryland.

Osborne Sprigg was a wealthy landowner who for several years represented Prince George's County in the Maryland House of Delegates. He and his cousin, Thomas Sprigg IV, were among the delegates who on April 28, 1788, signed the resolution by which the people of Maryland ratified the new U.S. Constitution that had been drafted by the Constitutional Congress meeting in Philadelphia in September 1787. Osborne's home, Northampton, was one of the more prestigious houses in Maryland at that time, with more than one thousand acres of prime agricultural land tended by slaves.

Almost nothing is known about Samuel Sprigg's early life, his brothers and sisters, his education, or his activities before he was elected governor of Maryland. Given his family's affluence, however, he presumably received an education appropriate for that period. He was almost certainly imbued with the social graces, family values, and sense of public service that characterized the ruling gentry of that era.

Two dates help establish benchmarks in Samuel's life. On January 11, 1811, when he was about twenty-seven and still living at Northampton, he married Violetta Lansdale, with whom he had two children. In 1815, on the death of his uncle Osborne, Samuel inherited Northampton, which would be his home for the rest of his life and the political base from which he rose to become the chief executive of Maryland.

Clouded though his early years may be, Samuel is known to have exhibited an early interest in politics. He followed in the footsteps of previous family members who in addition to serving as commissioners and delegates were also members of committees of correspondence and observation in 1774–75. Running as a Democrat, Samuel Sprigg was elected to the Maryland House of Delegates on October 4, 1819, winning his seat by the slimmest of margins. Nevertheless, when the delegates convened a few weeks later to form the new state government, they elected him Maryland's nineteenth governor. Subsequently reelected for second and third terms, he left office on December 16, 1822.

Historians have judged Governor Sprigg's administration to have been both vigorous and intelligent. A strong advocate of a statewide network of roads and canals, he staunchly supported the Chesapeake and Ohio Canal project. After leaving the governorship he was for a time president of the canal company's board.

History will remember him less kindly perhaps for his ruthless use of the political spoils system to solidify the Democratic Party's hold on the reins of power in the state. Shortly after assuming office he ordered the removal of virtually every officeholder who had been associated with the Federalist Party. Although quite controversial at the time, this action set the stage for his own reelection for two more terms and also ensured the election of other members of his ruling party to succeed him.

Samuel Sprigg died at his Prince George's County estate on April 21, 1855. Although initially buried at Saint Barnabas Church in Prince George's County, his daughter, Sarah, had his body reinterred in 1865 in the Carroll family mausoleum in Oak Hill Cemetery in Georgetown. His estate, valued at $50,000, included sixty-one slaves.[1]

In 1828 Sarah Sprigg, who was always called Sally, had married William Thomas Carroll. A handsome young man from a prestigious family, Carroll had been appointed clerk of the U.S. Supreme Court the previous year. Early in their marriage the couple lived in Georgetown, probably at Bellevue, Carroll's father's home at 2715 Q Street, N.W. But in 1835, when Governor Sprigg bought the Ringgold house at 1801 F Street, it was Sally and her husband who occupied it. While Sprigg was acknowledged as the owner of the house, everybody knew that he had purchased it for Sally. For the next sixty years it was known as the Carroll residence, even though the title remained in Sprigg's name until his death in 1855 and in trust to Sally until 1874.

In the late eighteenth and early nineteenth centuries, the Carroll family was one of America's largest and most prominent dynasties. There were so many of them that some members, including a long line of Charles Carrolls, became known by their places of residence. There was Charles Carroll of Annapolis, Charles Carroll of Carrollton, Charles Carroll of Bellevue, and Charles Carroll of Carrollsburg. They made large fortunes by combining the planting of export crops on their extensive plantations with such other profitable pursuits as merchandising, small manufacturing, land speculation, money lending, and law. Not only did they accumulate fortunes, they also acquired social and political preeminence as vestrymen, justices of the peace, council members, and delegates to assemblies. They often held public office during the early nation-building years of the Republic, thus demonstrating a willingness, as the historian Daniel Boorstin put it, to take on the burden of government and public responsibility.[2]

William Thomas Carroll, the son of Charles Carroll of Bellevue and the grandson of Charles Carroll of Carrollsburg, was born on Maryland's Eastern Shore, at Bellevue in Talbot County, on March 2, 1802. William's great-uncle Charles Carroll of Carrollton (1737–1832) was the last surviving signer of the Declaration of Independence, the foremost Roman Catholic in America, and arguably the wealthiest American of the period. Another uncle, the Jesuit Reverend John Carroll, S.J., was the first American-born Roman Catholic bishop in America and the founder of Georgetown University.[3]

After receiving what in the early nineteenth century was regarded as an ordinary English education, William Carroll was enrolled at the age of sixteen at Mount Saint Mary's College and Seminary in Emmitsburg, Maryland. It was there that young Carroll received a more classical education, graduating in 1822 at the age of twenty. Electing to prepare himself for a career in the legal profession, he subsequently studied law in Litchfield, Connecticut, where he was also admitted to the bar.[4]

Although Carroll lived his earliest years at Bellevue, he spent his more formative years in Washington, D.C. In 1813 his father purchased a large Federal-style mansion located at 2715 Q Street. The site had been part of an original tract known as the Rock of Dumbarton, patented in 1703 by Ninian Beall. Construction of the house on that site is believed to have been started in 1799 by Samuel Jackson but was completed in 1805 by Joseph Nource, the first registrar of the U.S. Treasury. When Charles Carroll bought the graciously columned red brick mansion in 1813, he renamed it Bellevue. That house, beautifully restored, is today the headquarters of the National Society of Colonial Dames of America, having been purchased in 1928 for that purpose and known since that time as Dumbarton House.[5]

It was to Bellevue on Q Street that William Carroll returned on completing law school. And it was in the nation's capital that he lived the rest of his life, fulfilling his legal ambitions by serving for thirty-six years as an officer of the U.S. Supreme Court. Like his Jesuit uncle, he played a major role in founding an institution of higher learning that still exists, although altered in name and form. With his good friend William Cranch, who had been reporter of the decisions of the Supreme Court and a justice of the Circuit Court of the District of Columbia, Carroll founded and taught part-time at a law school affiliated with Columbian College, forerunner of the George Washington University.

At the urging of Secretary of State Henry Clay, Chief Justice John Marshall appointed William Thomas Carroll the fifth clerk of the U.S. Supreme Court on January 28, 1827. While family connections may have sparked his initial consideration for the position, his actual appointment resulted from Marshall's satisfaction that he possessed the requisite

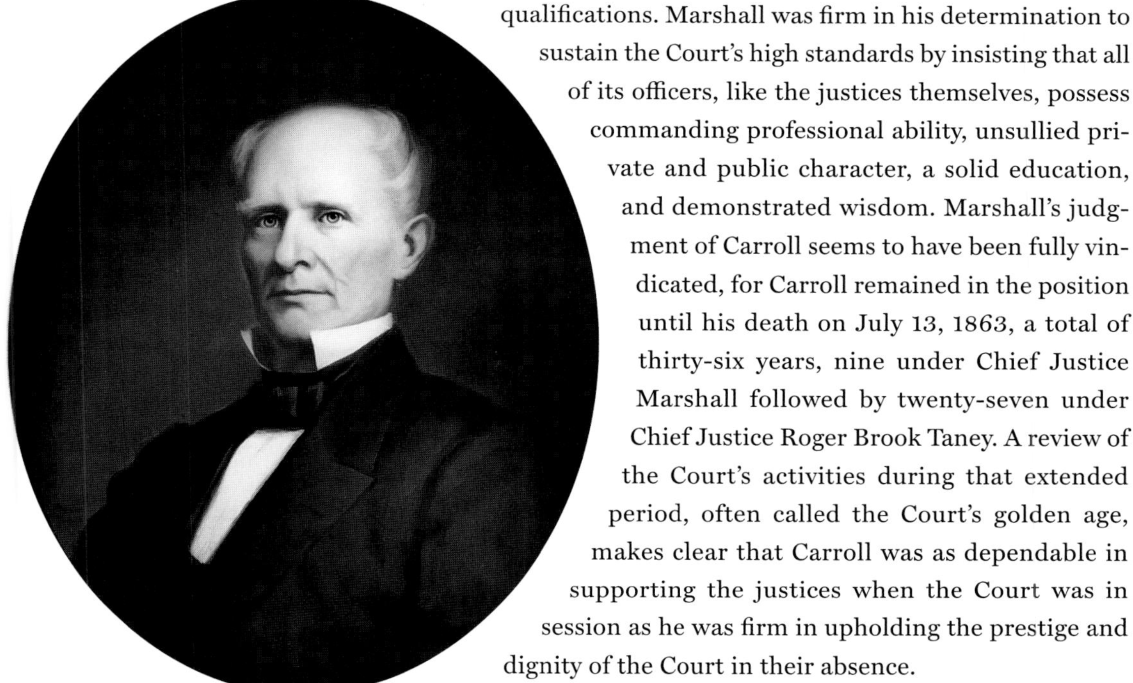

qualifications. Marshall was firm in his determination to sustain the Court's high standards by insisting that all of its officers, like the justices themselves, possess commanding professional ability, unsullied private and public character, a solid education, and demonstrated wisdom. Marshall's judgment of Carroll seems to have been fully vindicated, for Carroll remained in the position until his death on July 13, 1863, a total of thirty-six years, nine under Chief Justice Marshall followed by twenty-seven under Chief Justice Roger Brook Taney. A review of the Court's activities during that extended period, often called the Court's golden age, makes clear that Carroll was as dependable in supporting the justices when the Court was in session as he was firm in upholding the prestige and dignity of the Court in their absence.

William Thomas Carroll, clerk of the Supreme Court from 1827 to 1863, lived with his wife and family in the house from 1836 to 1863. His widow, Sarah Sprigg Carroll, remained until 1895. [Collection of the Supreme Court of the United States]

On Carroll's death, Chief Justice Taney noted: "When we are appointing a successor to Mr. Carroll, it is but justice to his memory to say that he was an accomplished and faithful officer, prompt and exact in business, and courteous in manner, and during the whole period of his judicial life discharged the duties of his office with justice to the public and the suitors, and to the entire satisfaction of every member of the Court."[6]

That William and Sally Carroll enjoyed a privileged and comfortable life is indisputable. Their enviable urban lifestyle was made possible by their individual wealth, their respective family connections and social prominence, and Carroll's advantage in holding a position of influence in government. The family's private fortune was significantly augmented by the fees Carroll collected for services rendered as clerk of the Court, even after deducting his office expenses. Just as consular officers in the early years of the Foreign Service were permitted to keep the fees they collected for processing consular invoices and the like, so too was Carroll authorized to retain the fees charged for his Court services. Surprisingly, this practice continued until 1964, when the clerk's position was put on salary and the expenses of the office were included in the Court's annual operating budget.[7]

During the entire period the Carrolls resided at 1801 F Street, from 1836 to 1895, it appears that they kept up a continuing round of hospitality that was said to have required two sets of servants, one for daytime and another for nighttime.[8] According to one former officer of the Supreme Court, the Carrolls, like many other wealthy Washingtonians, escaped each summer to Maryland's Eastern Shore. Accustomed to luxury, the family journeyed to and from the shore in an elegant carriage drawn by a team of matched horses. A vacationing associate justice of the Court, seeing their handsome rig parked in front of a fashionable beachfront social club, admired it and asked whose it was. Told it belonged to William Carroll, clerk of the Supreme Court, the inquiring justice reportedly said: "Perhaps I should exchange jobs with him; he obviously makes more money than I do."[9]

The Carrolls had four daughters and three sons. Violette Lansdale Carroll, born in 1829, married Dr. Thomas Swann Mercer, an ancestor of Lucy Mercer, who had a romance of thirty years with Franklin D. Roosevelt. Sally Carroll, born in 1837, was first married to Union Army Captain Charles Griffin in a ceremony attended by President and Mrs. Abraham Lincoln. After Griffin, by then a brigadier general, died of yellow fever, Sally married Count Maximilian Esterhazy, the Austro-Hungarian naval attaché, in a ceremony witnessed by President and Mrs. Ulysses S. Grant. Caroline Ann Carroll, born in 1841, married Union Navy Lieutenant T. Dix Belles; and the youngest Carroll daughter, Alida Catherine, born in 1842, married General John Marshall Brown.[10] Of the Carrolls' three sons, two died young. The surviving male, Samuel Sprigg Carroll, born in 1832, was graduated from West Point and fought with the Union forces in the battles of Cedar Mountain, Rapidan, Fredericksburg, Chancellorsville, Gettysburg, the Wilderness, and Spottsylvania. Seriously wounded, he retired as a major general in 1869.[11]

Of the Carroll family's sixty years in the F Street house, Sally Carroll spent the last thirty-two there as a widow. During their occupancy the Carrolls made many improvements. Early on, for example, they added a porch on the west side overlooking the garden. Exactly when the porch was added is not known, but a fire insurance map dated 1857 makes clear that at some time between 1835 and 1857 a fourteen-by-thirty-six-foot structure was built on that side. A porch, architectural historians suggest, would account for the house's expanded footprint. It is also interesting to note that the footprint shown in the 1857 map that includes the porch is exactly the same as the 1903 footprint, which shows a fourteen-by-thirty-six-foot wing added in 1896 by the Melville Fullers. The Fullers' architect, it seems, simply removed the porch and in its place constructed a four-story wing, the exact size as its base, which is still an integral part of the present-day house.

In the mid-1860s, at the midpoint of the Carroll era and shortly after William Carroll's death, a major renovation was begun that shaped the house's present appearance. The initial impetus for this expansion and renovation was the city's initiative in leveling many streets in preparation for installing water and sewer systems and paving the principal thoroughfares. Among the streets leveled were 18th and F Streets adjoining the Carroll residence. On both the south and east sides the streets were lowered about seven feet.[12]

With the house foundation threatened and exterior plantings exposed, Sally Carroll of necessity built the red brick, redstone-capped retaining wall that still encloses the property on the sides facing 18th and F Streets. Adjusting further to the new street level, she removed the outside front stairs that led from the old street level to the original second-floor entrance and created a new ground-floor entrance within a centered two-story, semioctagonal bay. Thereafter, guests entered the house through the new ground-floor front door and ascended an inside stairway that led to the second-floor entertainment rooms. With the carriage house and rear service area also left seven feet above the street level, a driveway and stairs were built at the back of the house off 18th Street to provide easy access.

At this juncture Sally Carroll also decided to improve the family's general living conditions by having the city's newly laid water, gas, and sewer lines connected to the house. She also elected to enhance the mansion's architectural elegance and expand its interior living space. To increase the interior footage from seven thousand to eight thousand square feet, the outer brick walls were extended straight up to create the present-day four-story Federal exterior with a flat roof.

Clearly visible on the 18th Street side of the house are the seams where the expertly laid Flemish-bond brick of the original gable-roofed attic meets the poorly laid, common-bond brick of the extended fourth floor.[13] The corresponding seams on the west side of the house are hidden from view by the four-story wing added in 1896 by the Melville Fullers. Quite visible across the front of the house are the seams where the new fourth floor and the semioctagonal entrance bay were added. Fortunately, these flaws are not noticeable to the casual observer and do not detract from the stately appearance of the house. Even today, despite decades of exposure to the elements, both the bricks laid in 1825 and those laid in the 1860s retain a rich red patina, just as the contrasting mortar retains its original cement-gray color.

Adding the two-story entrance bay and converting the partial attic to a full floor entailed realigning the window arrangement of the facade to achieve the architectural composition and balance characteristic of Federal-style structures. Brought into prominence at the second story of the new semioctagonal bay were three eleven-foot-tall windows, as conspicuous in the 1860s as the elaborate entrance had been at that position in 1825. Unfortunately, when viewed from the street the sills of these new windows were three feet below those of the adjoining windows in the south drawing and garden rooms.

The front entrance still boasts the wrought-iron lamp fixtures, railings, and balconies installed by the Carroll family in the 1860s. [DACOR Bacon House Foundation Collection]

Clearly needed for this all-important bank of five windows was a unifying horizontal line of sight. To provide it the two shorter windows were replaced with double-hung units that extended to the floor.[14] Thus lengthened to eleven feet, these altered windows had the appearance of French doors, an impression enhanced by the heavy center glazing bar dividing each window sash into two tall panes and by the wrought-iron balconies added on the outside. Inside, Dutch doors were installed at chair-rail height to give the interiors architectural symmetry and provide a measure of privacy and security. Following these adjustments, this sweep of five windows viewed in combination offered near-perfect scale and rhythm.

The third floor required no changes. The existing nine-foot windows, one each on the left and right sides, and a triple, side-by-side unit in the middle, with one full-size window flanked by two half-windows, already provided both consistency and harmony. On the expanded fourth floor, two matching seven-foot windows were installed on the left and right sides, offset in the center by a double side-by-side unit the same overall width as the triple window below it. The central window units on the third and fourth floors were slightly narrower than those in the bay but provided an appealing sense of lift and spatial unity at the upper levels.

Historians at the American Institute of Architects point out that in the early nineteenth century all Federal-style homes had shutters. In keeping with this custom Tench Ringgold in 1825 had installed working shutters on every window in the house. During the 1860s renovation Sally Carroll, recognizing the aesthetic value and weather-control benefits of these shutters, wisely elected to retain them. Her changes established a pleasingly hierarchical fenestration, with the seven-foot windows and recessed front door on the ground floor successively topped by eleven-foot windows on the second floor, nine-foot windows on the third, and seven-foot windows on the fourth.

By having stylistically identical, boldly framed, and uniformly glazed windows in three vertical columns, all sills and window headers in alignment, and paired shutters on every unit, an almost flawless horizontal and vertical symmetry was achieved. This arrangement not only avoided proportional discord, it also minimized the otherwise boxy appearance of a structure almost forty-five feet square at its base and fifty feet high. Notwithstanding the ornamented cornice Alice Copley Thaw added to the roof crown and the bay in 1911, the facade presents an aesthetically pleasant combination of Federal-style influences. The sure sense of proportion and the rhythmic detailing create an appealing appearance of architectural unity.

The laying of natural gas lines throughout the principal areas of the city in the 1860s made possible the installation of the matching gaslight-and-candle chandeliers in the two drawing rooms and the adjoining dining room. Gaslights had been installed in the White House as early as 1848, and many wealthy families, the Carrolls among them, followed that example as soon as a dependable supply of natural gas became available. The gaslights were a great convenience, one that also added a note of elegance to the rooms used for public entertaining. The chandeliers Sally Carroll installed, two eight-branch and one six-branch fixtures, were made in Philadelphia about 1840. Still gracing the principal entertainment rooms, and still used with candles, these fire-gilded antique fixtures remain in their original nonelectrified state.

The carriage house at the back of the house, still extant, was begun by Sally Carroll in the 1860s. After tearing down the two outbuildings erected by Ringgold in 1825, she built a single two-story, all-brick structure, which still forms the rear and largest portion of the existing carriage house. Hugging the north property line, as did Ringgold's barns, this section is situated far enough back from 18th Street to be clear of the house on both its north and west sides.

Unchanged since the 1860s are the gaslight chandeliers installed by Sally Carroll. They remain nonelectrified but are now used with candles. [DACOR Bacon House Foundation Collection]

Later, probably in the 1880s, the second Carroll-era section was built. Still standing, it is the narrow rectangular arm that stretches along the north boundary, beginning at the 18th Street property line and extending westward to the top of the current driveway. The brick used in this later section is noticeably inferior in both color and texture, and the workmanship leaves much to be desired when compared with that of the main house.

The third section of the carriage house was built in 1896 by the Melville Fullers and joins the two sections built by Sally Carroll. In 1911 a new owner, Alice Copley Thaw, built a fourth section to give the overall structure greater uniformity and symmetry. This last addition marked the transition from the horse-and-carriage era to that of the combustion-engine automobile and created the carriage house footprint as we know it today.

In the course of building and enlarging the carriage house in four stages over a period of fifty years, numerous other changes were made. At different times new doors were opened in old walls, existing doors widened, and new windows knocked through walls to provide better light and ventilation. These alterations are clearly identifiable by the contrasting color and texture of the brick and mortar used in the different construction periods, just as telltale lines reveal where each new section joined an old one. In an effort to hide the most noticeable blemishes, some sections of the structure were painted a dark brick red, probably in 1896 but possibly as late as 1911. While much of the red stain has faded, it is still quite pronounced in places.

As one would expect, architectural historians and concerned preservationists delight in the existence of these imperfections since they help determine facts of the construction history. Moreover, they regard as wholly appropriate some external variegation in a building whose several sections were built piecemeal over a forty-five year period. Today, mellowed by time, the carriage house has a unique charm. Although diminutive by comparison with the adjoining mansion, it provides well-proportioned, clean-lined offices large enough to provide a most desirable rental property and a source of income for the DACOR Bacon House Foundation. Outside, the patchwork of architectural detail gives the structure an old, somewhat exotic appearance that adds interest and a note of historical authenticity to the historic premises.

As noted earlier, when Governor Sprigg died in 1855, title to the property passed to his daughter, Sally Sprigg Carroll, but only in trust. Confirming his original intention that the house would be Sally's alone, Sprigg named as trustees three friends—Daniel W. Middleton, Alex H. Lawrence, and James M. Carlisle—who for the next twenty years protected her interest in the property. Not until 1874 after Congress passed the Married Woman's Act, which for the first time permitted a wife to hold property free of her husband, was title to the property formally transferred to Sally.[15]

William Carroll died in 1863 at age sixty-one, but Sally Carroll lived on in the house until her death, at age eighty-one, in 1895. Both are buried in the Carroll family mausoleum in Oak Hill Cemetery in Georgetown. During the four years that Abraham Lincoln and his wife, Mary, lived in the White House, they maintained a close friendship with the Carrolls. That friendship explains why President and Mrs. Lincoln were occasional guests in the Carroll home and attended their daughter Sally's wedding to Captain Griffin. It also explains why Lincoln's son William Wallace Lincoln, called Willie, who died in Washington on February 20, 1862, was interred for three years in the Carroll family mausoleum. Often recounted are the stories of President Lincoln's frequent visits to the cemetery to spend many hours in quiet contemplation at his son's grave. When in 1864, following his assassination at Ford's Theater, Lincoln's body was taken by train to Springfield, Illinois, for burial, Willie's coffin was carried home on the same train.[16]

78

CHAPTER FIVE

ANOTHER CHIEF JUSTICE HOLDS COURT

1896–1910

The front entrance to 1801 F Street, about 1930, shows the bay windows and balconies installed in the mid-1860s and the semielliptical bay adapted during the Fuller era. [DACOR Bacon House Foundation Collection]

FOLLOWING Sally Sprigg Carroll's death, General John Marshall Brown, her son-in-law and the executor of her will, sold the Carroll residence on April 13, 1896, to Mary Ellen Fuller. Known to her friends as Mollie, the former Mary Ellen Coolbaugh of Chicago was the wife of Melville Weston Fuller, the sitting chief justice of the U.S. Supreme Court. Nominated by President Grover Cleveland on April 30, 1888, Fuller was sworn in as the Court's eighth chief justice on October 8 of the same year.

On arriving in the nation's capital in 1888, the Fullers temporarily rented a turreted stone house called Belmont near the end of the 14th Street streetcar line. Within a few months, however, Mollie Fuller found and purchased as the family's permanent residence a large brick house at 1800 Massachusetts Avenue, N.W., just east of Dupont Circle. In 1896, seeking a more distinguished home in the quieter and more fashionable area near the White House, she bought the mansion at 1801 F Street, where the family would live for the next fourteen years.[1]

Melville Fuller was born in Augusta, Maine, on February 11, 1822, to Frederick A. Fuller, a promising young lawyer, and his wife, the former Catharine Martin Weston. Melville's maternal grandfather was Nathan Weston Jr., at the time one of the three justices of the Maine Supreme

Court. The marriage of Frederick and Catharine on May 31, 1830, was one of the social highlights of the year in Augusta, uniting two equally prominent Maine families. The Fullers traced their ancestry to one of the forty-one signers of the Mayflower Compact, Edward Fuller, who with his wife, Ann, arrived in America on the *Mayflower* in November 1620. The first Westons arrived in 1640. Family members on both sides, through several generations, had achieved professional success and demonstrated public responsibility as lawyers, jurists, educators, physicians, military leaders, authors, governors, and a U.S. senator.[2]

Given their family connections, the young couple settled into what appeared to be an idyllic life. A son, Henry, was born in 1831, followed by a second son, Melville, two years later.[3] However, just three months after Melville's birth, Catharine filed for divorce, alleging that her husband had committed adultery beginning two months after the nuptials. Although Frederick denied the charges as alleged, the divorce was quickly granted with Catharine gaining custody of the two young children.

Seeking solace and support, Catharine and the two boys made their home for the next several years with her parents, Nathan and Paulina Weston, in Augusta. It was inevitable in these circumstances, but perhaps fortunate in the end, that the Westons would play an important role in Melville's upbringing. Nevertheless, the strong-willed Catharine, determined to be the primary force in shaping her sons' interests and character, began giving piano lessons to earn the money needed to maintain a measure of independence and provide for the boys' schooling. When Catharine remarried in 1844 and went to live near Bangor with her new husband, the Westons' influence increased considerably and became dominant. Young Melville, then eleven, seemingly unable to reconcile himself either to the new state of family affairs or to life in Bangor with his stepfather, returned to Augusta to live most of the time thereafter with his grandparents. During these formative years the Westons, a strict couple, would push Melville into avidly reading the books in Justice Weston's fine library, thus setting firmly in place his life-long scholarly habits.[4]

Given grandfather Weston's scholarly ways and his new high station as the chief justice of the Maine Supreme Court, it is difficult to imagine that he would not agree to send Melville to college. Yet, refuse he did, and for a time it appeared that young Fuller would have to forgo the advantage of a higher education. Fortunately, his mother and his grandmother Weston thought otherwise. Convinced that Melville had a bright future and that a college education was essential to enable him to fulfill his destiny, they secretly conspired to provide the funds that permitted him to enter Bowdoin College in 1849. Just sixteen when admitted, he was a serious and outstanding student and received his A.B. degree with honors in September 1853.

After graduation Fuller read law for one year in the Bangor law offices of his uncles, Nathan Weston and George Melville, and then attended Harvard Law School for six months.[5] This Harvard experience, which he tended to belittle, gave him the distinction of being the first chief justice of the United States to have any formal law school training.[6] After being admitted to the bar in Maine in 1855 and clerking for a few months in the office of his uncle Nathan, Fuller returned to Augusta. Once there he opened his own law practice and with another uncle, Benjamin Fuller, shared the editorship of the *Age*, the state's principal Democratic newspaper.[7]

Seemingly settled in Augusta, Fuller flirted briefly with politics in 1856 by winning election as one of three aldermen for Augusta's Sixth Ward. One week later, when the Augusta Common Council was formed, he was elected its president and city solicitor. While momentarily excited about his adventure into politics, he quickly became disillusioned. Two months later, dissatisfied with his life and depressed over his failed four-year betrothal to Susan Robinson, he decided to move to Chicago. Like thousands of others he took advantage of the newly opened railroad linking the eastern seaboard to the West and sought a fresh start in the Midwest's most exciting city. Among those who shared that adventure and became successful were Marshall Field and George M. Pullman.[8]

In Chicago Jane Reynolds's modest boarding house on Wabash Avenue became Fuller's first home. It was a circumstance that would have important consequences for him in short order. Her husband, Eri Reynolds, who had died in 1851, had been the owner of a small meatpacking plant. He also owned several parcels of real estate located in what would become the famous Chicago Loop. These would prove quite valuable for his heirs, including, eventually, Fuller.

In frequent letters to his family, Fuller complained about his tiny seven-by-nine-foot-room. He also complained about the food, describing the soup as tasting like "refuse from a tanyard, the roast beef like sole leather, and the potatoes like boiled cobblestones." Trying though these living conditions may have been, they were gratifyingly offset by the presence of Calista, Reynolds's lovely daughter. To his mother Fuller wrote:

"She has glossy, luxuriant hair, . . . wears pretty boots [and] neat hats and exhibits some considerable taste in her toilet generally." To Calista, he sometimes expressed his growing affection in sonnets, and for his effort he claimed to have received pleasant payment in the form of "a contact with lips that are soft in the hall." Drawn to each other, Fuller and Calista Ophelia Reynolds were married on June 28, 1858. Their few years together were happy ones, but tragically Calista contracted tuberculosis and died in the fall of 1864 shortly after the birth of their second daughter.[9]

In his early professional years Fuller found politics irresistible. He belonged to and was an officer of several Democratic Party organizations, and he was also a delegate to several Democratic Party conventions. Participation in state and national political rallies was a passion, and he eagerly accepted invitations to speak at political forums. On only two occasions, however, did he dabble in Chicago's political wars as a candidate. In 1861 he was elected one of the four delegates to represent Chicago at a convention called to frame a new constitution for Illinois. The following year he won a seat in the Illinois state legislature. Although he was admired for his legal skills and oratory and was an acknowledged leader of his party, he chose at the end of his first legislative term to return to private law practice. Throughout the rest of his life his interest in politics would remain high, but his participation would always be in support of others and never again as a candidate.[10]

In 1865 Fuller received an unexpected financial windfall when, to widen Dearborn Street, the city of Chicago sought the land that Calista had inherited from her father and then left to Melville. Using his considerable legal skills to full advantage, Fuller seized this opportunity and negotiated a sizable payment for the crucial property. With this money, plus an additional $55,000 he was able to borrow, he began a portfolio of real estate investments, beginning with the construction of the five-story Reynolds office building, one of the largest structures in Chicago at the time. When it was completed, Fuller moved his thriving and expanding law office into it and rented out space to several of the city's foremost law firms. There he prospered until 1871, when the Chicago fire destroyed the building and all of his books and files.[11] In a sense he had to start all over again, but not quite from scratch.

Luckily for Fuller, a most fortuitous turning point in his life had occurred a few years before the disastrous fire. Seeking a more suitable residential neighborhood in which to raise his two daughters, he moved to a

Melville Weston Fuller resided in the house from 1896 to 1910. Fuller served as chief justice of the U.S. Supreme Court from 1888 until 1910. His portrait was painted by Robert Hinckley. [Collection of the Supreme Court of the United States]

home on South Wabash Avenue. His next-door neighbor was William F. Coolbaugh, president of both the Union National Bank of Chicago and the Chicago Clearing House and probably the most important banker in the Midwest. The two men soon became good friends, and inevitably the thirty-three-year-old Fuller met Coolbaugh's vivacious twenty-one-year-old daughter, Mary Ellen. It was a love-at-first-sight meeting, of which he said: "This is a love match. . . . I was introduced to her on a Saturday, with her the next Saturday, and engaged the Wednesday after."[12] They were married in May 1866 and, following an extended honeymoon in Europe, took up residence in a large home given to Mary Ellen as a wedding present by her father. There, in relative luxury, they raised Fuller's two daughters by his first wife and their own seven daughters and one son, born between 1868 and 1880. Despite the fire, Fuller had his clients and a financial rock—the Coolbaughs—to stand on.

By 1877, two decades after his arrival in Chicago, Fuller was a successful and contented man. Behind him were the years of struggle to establish his law practice, the political battles, his first wife's illness and death, and the disastrous Chicago fire. He could well afford all of life's necessities and many of its luxuries, and his domestic life, thanks to his successful second marriage, was blissful.[13]

In the 1884 presidential elections Fuller vigorously supported Grover Cleveland, who, after becoming president, tried repeatedly to entice his longtime friend into government service. During his first year in office Cleveland offered Fuller the chairmanship of the Civil Service Commission, the post of solicitor general, and the chance to fill one of the three seats on the U.S. Pacific Railway Commission. All overtures were rejected. In 1888 the death of Chief Justice Morrison R. Waite gave Cleveland the chance to nominate Fuller to the country's highest judicial position. Both flattered and delighted, he accepted the honor and was sworn in as chief justice on October 8, 1888.[14]

Willard L. King, in his excellent biography of Fuller, writes that Fuller

inherited from the Westons his "sensitivity and conscientiousness, his gentleness and kindliness, and his capacity for methodical work and monklike study; from the Fuller side, his passionate and romantic traits, his independence of judgment and his genius for friendship." That Fuller possessed a deep intellectual bent is beyond doubt. He was clearly a man of strong moral conviction and as a lifelong Episcopalian embraced religion as an integral facet of everyday life. While occasionally exhibiting a quiet, gentle sense of humor, his demeanor in most situations reflected his disciplined New England upbringing. Despite spending several decades away from his beloved Maine, he always spoke of the continuity of life in Augusta as having greatly influenced and stabilized his life.[15]

Fuller believed that the Bill of Rights was the most important part of the Constitution and that the best government is that which governs least. His political philosophy was "sound money, free trade, states' rights, no paternalism, governmental economy, and the preservation of the civil rights of the individual."[16] His personal philosophy, instilled in him by his grandmother Weston, was, "Don't come forward too soon, get knowledge and experience to stand upon like a rock—then if the wind beats upon you, you won't fall." Perhaps never quite understanding Melville's mind-set, she also advised, "Don't go against Freedom."[17]

During his twenty-two years on the Court, Fuller established a distinguished judicial record. Many of his court colleagues, among them Oliver Wendell Holmes, as well as many court historians, judged him to be the best presiding judge ever. More often than not he enjoyed the support of most of his fellow justices when reaching decisions. In more than four thousand votes, on a ratio of two to one, the majority of the justices voted as he did. Over the years he wrote more than eight hundred opinions, and scholars generally agree that they were models of vigorous expression and direct reasoning that used with good effect allusions to history, classical literature, and the Bible.[18]

Chief Justice Melville Weston Fuller's court posed in October 1898. Fuller, who lived at 1801 F Street from 1896 to 1910, is seated in the center. Associate Justice Edward D. White Jr., whose grandfather, Tench Ringgold, built the house in 1825, is in the back row, second from the right. [Collection of the Supreme Court of the United States]

The case of *Pollock v. Farmer's Loan and Trust Company,* for which he wrote the majority opinion in 1895, is the decision for which he is probably best remembered. In that verdict he stated forcefully that the federal government had no right, as promulgated in the Income Tax Law of 1894, to put a tax on personal income. That view prevailed until February 25, 1913, when the Sixteenth Amendment of the Constitution was ratified.[19]

As the 1892 national elections approached, many of the Democratic Party's most influential members had grave doubts that Grover Cleveland, who had been out of the White House for four years, could be reelected for a second term. Fuller, they argued, was a much stronger candidate, and they urged him to stand for the party's nomination. Even though his wife strongly supported the idea, Fuller refused the overtures and instead backed Cleveland, who was reelected. As one of his first acts in forming a cabinet, a grateful President-elect Cleveland turned to Fuller and offered him a chance if he resigned from the Supreme Court to be his secretary of state. While flattered, Fuller asked that he be allowed "to decline the great place you were kind enough to wish me to accept," adding that he thought "the surrender of the highest judicial office in the world for a political position, even though so eminent, would detract from the dignity and weight of the tribunal."[20] An old friend, Judge Walter Q. Gresham, was appointed in his place.

When the Fullers acquired the house at 1801 F Street in 1896, they engaged the noted architect John McGregor to enlarge and modernize it. Giving priority to the family's need for more living space, McGregor added a fourteen-by-thirty-six-foot, four-story wing on the west side of the house, in the exact location where at midcentury the Carrolls had built a porch the same size. This new wing increased the interior space of the house from eight thousand to ten thousand square feet and accommodated a separate service staircase, additional bedrooms and bathrooms, and a butler's pantry. The pantry adjoined the dining room and was connected to the basement kitchen by a dumbwaiter. The new wing also accommodated a small residential-size elevator, a cable unit driven by an electric motor, which survived until 1986 when DACOR replaced it with a modern twelve-person elevator.

Having given up the west porch to accommodate the construction of the new wing, the Fullers decided to build a replacement porch on the north side of the house. In sultry Washington at the turn of the century, a porch was essential for comfortable summer living. Larger than the unit it replaced, the new porch (now known as the gallery) measured forty-four feet by nine feet and added four hundred square feet of living space. Its utility was enhanced by floor-to-ceiling glass outer walls on three sides. In addition, a coal-burning Franklin stove was added, making the porch quite livable much of the year. Access to the north porch from the adjoining drawing and dining rooms was through Dutch doors over which oversized, double-hung windows had been installed, thus matching in size and architectural effect the windows and arches throughout the adjacent entertainment rooms. From the garden the porch was accessible by an outside stair.

The front facade of the house, substantially altered by Sally Carroll in the mid-1860s, was further altered by the Fullers when the architect changed the two-story semioctagonal bay to a semielliptical one. This change, everyone agreed, gave the entrance and the entire front facade a softer and more inviting look. Inside, the central staircase was aggrandized by installing lead-camed windows in the front door and its adjoining side panels, as well as in the door and paired side panels that separated the staircase from the rear service facilities at the back of the ground-floor vestibule. Unadorned until this time, the staircase walls were embellished with the sheathing of a high-paneled wooden wainscot.[21]

During the Carroll era the rear half of the ground floor was essentially two large rooms. When McGregor partitioned this space for the Fullers, it

The north porch, now called the gallery, was added by the Fullers in 1896. It replaced the west porch, which was demolished to accommodate a four-story addition. [DACOR Bacon House Foundation Collection]

became a kitchen, furnace room, storeroom, and butler's bedroom and bath.[22] The latest comfort-giving and energy-saving mechanical devices were installed as a part of the modernization effort. The kitchen was equipped with a massive new stove suitable for preparing banquet-size meals, as well as a battery of counters and sinks sufficient to service a large family and a busy entertainment schedule. In the new furnace room a large boiler was installed to provide central heat.

To enhance the appeal of the entertainment rooms and the family bedrooms, McGregor incorporated many eye-pleasing architectural changes. The fireplace mantel and surround installed in the butler's bedroom in 1896 is still used in a reconfigured room that is DACOR's Battle-Torbert library. Still in use are the fireplace mantel and surround in the Fuller bedroom. When this bedroom unit was removed in 1986 to be repaired and refinished, a penciled note was found scratched on the back. It read: "RUSH, Chief Justice Fuller, 1896." In William Seale's 1975 book *The Tasteful Interlude* is a picture of the principal drawing room at 1801 F Street as it appeared following the Fullers' remodeling.[23]

The Fullers also enlarged the carriage house by constructing a brick addition that linked the two detached sections the Carrolls had built some years earlier. This added space provided better accommodations for the family's horses and storage for their carriages. It also included modest living quarters for the attending coachman.

Because he was the ranking jurist in the land, Chief Justice Fuller naturally held a high position in Washington's official society. As a consequence, he and his wife were entertained frequently and, as expected, reciprocated with appropriate dinners and receptions. Mollie Fuller reveled in the social whirl and graciously participated in every formal aspect of it. By contrast, the chief justice participated more as a duty. Given a choice he would have stayed home to read a book. In time, the combined strain of his social life and the pressure of his court responsibilities began to affect his health. Often feeling overwhelmed, he was reminded time and again of the rumor that his predecessor, Chief Justice Morrison R. Waite, had been killed by excessive dining out. Not surprisingly, there came the moment when he was obliged to restrict his social engagements and, later, when he found it necessary to refuse virtually all invitations. One can speculate that Fuller's retirement from the social scene began a trend that, to some degree, continues to this day—that of Supreme Court justices' limiting their involvement in official Washington social activities.[24]

Notwithstanding the chief justice's retirement from the general social scene, the Fullers continued to host small dinners to entertain the other justices, particularly the new court appointees, of whom there were fourteen during Fuller's more than two decades on the court. They also enjoyed hosting dinner parties for their close friends, among whom were President and Mrs. Cleveland, and the William Howard Tafts, initially when Taft was solicitor general and later when he was secretary of war. Occasionally welcomed to their home as well were other cabinet members and congressional leaders, particularly members of the Senate Judiciary Committee.

What Fuller regarded as promiscuous society was carefully avoided, as was ostentatious entertaining. While his $10,500 annual salary made elaborate entertaining impossible, his income from real estate holdings in Chicago, together with Mollie Fuller's independent financial means, permitted them to enjoy a privileged lifestyle.[25]

The lifestyle that they and others of similar fortune and position could enjoy is eloquently evoked by passages from Lois Sprigg Hazell's undated and unpublished manuscript, found among Virginia Bacon's personal papers, describing a visit to the Fuller house at the turn of the century:

> The closed carriage waited at the door, and the two bay horses, Tommy and Tomkins, seemed to be smoking as their warm breath puffed into the cold air of a Washington January afternoon. After helping mother into the black box-like vehicle, Young, the coachman, lifted me onto the seat beside her saying: "Now, lovey, you be a good little girl and sit still beside your ma while we drive."
>
> On this winter afternoon mother and I were going calling. Like all mothers, mine enjoyed showing the relatives her first child, a precocious three-year-old. As a family photograph shows, I was dressed in my best new winter coat of pale tan broadcloth with a velvet collar and matching hat and, joy of joys, a tiny fur

The lines of the original roof before the Fuller-era alterations can be seen in the subtle variation in brick visible in this photograph from around 1930. [DACOR Bacon House Foundation Collection]

muff hung around my neck on a silk cord. I also had a real purse with several bright pennies in it, and to my sorrow, the outfit included kid gloves that had to be worked on over uncooperative little fingers.

Our destination was the home of mother's cousins, the Melville Fullers. Cousin Melville was the Chief Justice of the United States from 1888 to 1910. After a clippity-clop trip down 18th Street, the carriage drew up in front of the familiar red brick house at 1801 F Street. Earlier, from 1835 to 1849, the house had belonged to my father's relative, Samuel Sprigg, who from 1819 to 1822 had been the nineteenth governor of Maryland, and until 1896 to his daughter, Mrs. William Thomas Carroll (née Sarah Sprigg). Now it was my mother's family who lived there.

On that long ago afternoon a white-capped maid opened the front door holding a small silver tray on which mother deposited the usual visiting cards, one of hers and two of my father's. We were ushered into the parlor where I obeyed instructions to shake hands with Cousin Mary and another guest, and I gave each a little bob that passed for the curtsey expected by older women. With my coat unbuttoned, I was placed on a low stool to one side of my mother's chair where I began the tedious job of getting off the hated kid gloves. Seeing me busily occupied, mother turned her attention to the two ladies and became engrossed in grown-up conversation. Suddenly, aware of an unnatural silence on my part, mother glanced down. Her little darling had taken off not only the gloves, hat, coat, shoes and stockings, but was tugging with promising success at the dress with the evident intention of removing everything. The visit was definitely at an end.[26]

Chief Justice Fuller was especially pleased to live in the house where Chief Justice John Marshall and several members of his court had lived. He often voiced his pride in holding his weekly court conferences in the same rooms at 1801 F Street where Marshall's court had deliberated in 1831–32. Always convened on Saturday, the weekly conference of the nine justices was of extreme importance to Fuller, and he preferred to hold them in the comfort and privacy of his home, rather than, as had been the custom, in the old Senate Chamber in the south wing of the Capitol or at a table set among the book stacks of the Supreme Court Library. It was at these weekly conferences that Fuller began the custom, followed to this day, of having the nine justices shake hands before beginning their deliberations. Over the years, those attending his weekly conferences at 1801 F Street were Associate Justices Horace Gray, David J. Brewer, Henry B. Brown, George Shiras Jr., Edward D. White Jr. (grandson of Tench Ringgold), Rufus W. Peckham, Joseph McKenna, Oliver Wendell Holmes Jr., William R. Ray, William H. Moody, Horace H. Lurton, and Charles Evans Hughes.[27]

Each year it was the Fullers' custom to spend the summer at their home in Sorrento, Maine, and it was there in 1904 that Mollie Fuller, twelve years younger than her husband, died of a heart attack. Following the funeral services her body was sent to Chicago for burial. After her death Chief Justice Fuller's interest and energies declined sharply, to a point where President Theodore Roosevelt tried to talk him into retirement. He seemed always depressed, was often too ill to take part in court deliberations, and was constantly concerned that the Court's business seemed perpetually in arrears. Moreover, he missed his children, who were scattered in Tarrytown, New York, Tacoma, Washington, and Chicago, and worried that one or more of them was on the brink of being distressingly ill. He missed seeing most of his grandchildren grow up. Only the Mason children, his daughter Jane Fuller Mason's children, who lived in Washington, D.C., were at hand, and he looked forward to their frequent visits to 1801 F Street and the summer home in Sorrento.

In 1910 Fuller went to Maine for his usual summer respite. After his customary visit to church on Sunday, July 3, he called his daughter Jane in the evening to say that he was quite ill. In the early hours of July 4 he suffered a heart attack and died. Like Thomas Jefferson, John Adams, and James Monroe, he died on the birthday of the country he had so loyally and ably served as chief justice. Following services in Sorrento, where he was remembered as the most beloved of all chief justices, he was buried in Chicago next to Mollie.[28]

To fill the vacancy created by Fuller's death, President Theodore Roosevelt appointed Edward D. White Jr. chief justice in 1910. As recounted in the Ringgold family history, White became an associate justice of the U.S. Supreme Court in 1894. This circumstance is of special interest because his mother was the former Catherine Ringgold, who lived at 1801 F Street for ten years and whose wedding reception, following her marriage to Congressman Edward Douglass White Sr., was held in the house. It was Chief Justice White's maternal grandfather, Tench Ringgold, who had built the home in 1824–25. During the period 1896–1910, Justice White must have derived great pleasure in visiting his mother's and grandfather's old home to attend the weekly conferences of the justices forming the Fuller court. He thus joined his predecessors, John Marshall and Melville Fuller, as the third chief justice to be closely associated with the house and add luster to its history.

In 1911, several months after Chief Justice Fuller's death, the mansion at 1801 F Street was sold to Alice Copley Thaw.

CHAPTER SIX

RENOVATION AND NEW RESIDENTS

1911–1923

The dining room received a faux-marble cornice to hide indirect lighting as part of the renovation during Alice Thaw's residence. [DACOR Bacon House Foundation Collection]

ALICE CORNELIA COPLEY THAW was the daughter and heir of William Thaw (1818–89), a Pittsburgh capitalist and philanthropist who had made a huge fortune in steamships, railroads, and mining. After attending Western University in Pennsylvania, now the University of Pittsburgh, Thaw traveled throughout the Ohio Valley as a clerk for the U.S. Bank of Philadelphia, collecting overdue debts for the bank. Traveling mostly on horseback, he quickly realized the need for more comfortable and faster transportation facilities. Just as quickly he recognized the business opportunity offered to whoever would provide them.

At the age of twenty-three, he and his brother-in-law, Thomas S. Clarke, formed a transportation company that operated canal portages and steamboat lines offering service from major eastern cities to New Orleans. From this modest beginning in 1841 he expanded his interests until in his mid-thirties he controlled more than 150 steamboats. In 1855, with characteristic foresight, he sold his shipping interests and shifted his investments to railroads. In the ensuing years he became a powerful force in rail transport as an officer, director, and owner of various lines that linked the industrial and population centers of the eastern seaboard. At their peak his railway interests stretched westward as far as St. Louis.[1]

In 1841 Thaw married Eliza Blair, with whom he fathered five children.

The dining room, like both drawing rooms on the second floor, received a black marble mantel and surrounds during the Thaw renovation. [DACOR Bacon House Foundation Collection]

Four years after her death in 1861 he married Mary Sibbert Copley and fathered five more children, one of whom was Alice Copley Thaw. Another was Harry L. Thaw, the playboy who murdered the architect Stanford White in Madison Square Garden in an *affaire d'amour* over Thaw's wife, the former chorus girl and famed beauty Evelyn Nesbitt.[2]

Alice Thaw inherited a sizable fortune when her father died in 1889. Like many other wealthy American debutantes, she sought and found romance with a titled, although poor, foreigner. In 1903 in a lavish ceremony held in Pittsburgh Alice married George Francis Alexander (Seymour), the earl of Yarmouth, and took up residence in England. When the marriage failed (it was annulled) in 1908, she returned to the United States and in 1911 bought the house at 1801 F Street from the estate of Chief Justice Fuller.[3]

With the assistance of the architect Jules Henri de Sibour, Alice Copley Thaw, as she preferred to be called, remodeled and improved the interior of the house. In the dining room she had a faux-marble Georgian cornice installed, behind which indirect lighting was hidden. Black marble surrounds and mantels were mounted on the three fireplaces in the drawing and dining rooms, and a white marble surround and mantel were added to the fireplace in the master bedroom. New bathrooms were created on the two upper floors. To facilitate the large-scale entertaining she planned, Thaw also had de Sibour enlarge the arch between the two drawing rooms, as well as the arch between the dining room and the adjoining north drawing room. To further enhance the flow between the principal entertainment rooms she had de Sibour replace the dining room's hinged doors with pocket doors. Mounted on tracks, these doors could be pushed out of the way into corresponding wall pockets.

During this renovation all of the plumbing was replaced and a full-scale electric lighting system was installed for the first time. The elaborate Georgian-style metal cornice on the roof and the matching cornice on the front portico were also added at that time.[4] In addition, the adjoining carriage house, with its twenty-five hundred square feet of space, was enlarged and modernized. To simplify real property records, Thaw had the three original F Street lots—nos. 1, 2, and 15—consolidated into a single lot—no. 24, square 142 (Liber 44, Folio 186).

In 1912 Thaw married Geoffrey Whitney of New York and Boston. Because the couple intended to divide their time between homes in New York and Connecticut, Alice Whitney elected to retain 1801 F Street but rent it to others. Over the next decade it was occupied by Adolph C. and Mary Miller, Harold and Alonsita Walker, Ruth and Joseph Medill McCormick, and lastly Robert Low and Virginia Murray Bacon.[5]

Adolph Miller was a nationally recognized economist who taught at the University of California, Cornell University, University of Chicago, and Harvard University before coming to Washington in 1913 to serve as assistant to Secretary of the Interior Franklin K. Lane and concurrently as director of the national parks. When the Federal Reserve Board was created in 1914, President Woodrow Wilson appointed Miller one of its initial members.

The Millers lived at 1801 F Street for two years, from 1913 to 1915. When they first rented the house, the block across the street, bounded by E and F Streets and 18th and 19th Streets, had been Jerome Park.[6] Construction soon began there on the Department of the Interior, at the time the second-largest building in the United States, and the noise and confusion led the Millers to move out within two years. (The General Services Administration occupies the building today.)

The Millers sublet the house to Harold Walker, an internationally known lawyer who had a long association with oil interests in Mexico and California. In Washington he led the fight by oil importers to forestall congressional imposition of a tariff on petroleum imports.[7]

From 1917 to 1919 the house was rented to Ruth and Joseph Medill McCormick. McCormick, who had just been elected senator from Illinois, was the brother of Colonel Robert McCormick, owner of the *Chicago Tribune*. Ruth McCormick was the daughter of Mark Hanna, the legendary midwestern political wheeler-dealer. The McCormicks occupied the house when the League of Nations debate was raging in Washington, and the senator's strong opposition to the League and to the Versailles Treaty reportedly sparked many lively discussions at their dinner parties.[8]

CHAPTER SEVEN

THE BACONS HOST THE CAPITAL

1923–1980

IN THE NATIONAL ELECTIONS of 1922, Robert Low Bacon, running as a Republican from New York's First District, won election to the U.S. House of Representatives by a substantial majority. Arriving in the nation's capital early in 1923, he and his wife, Virginia Murray Bacon, rented the stately house at 1801 F Street for their residence. After he was reelected two years later they bought the house on March 27, 1925.[1]

The earliest recorded member of Robert Low Bacon's family, Nathaniel Bacon, was born in Cornwall, England, and immigrated to America in 1639. From that beginning an unbroken line of sons ran through six generations to Captain Daniel Carpenter Bacon, Representative Bacon's great-grandfather, a Boston-based shipowner involved in the Pacific trade. The captain's son, William Benjamin Bacon, was a trader and banker who married Emily Crosby Low. Their son, Robert (Representative Bacon's father), was a banker, soldier, and diplomat who married Martha Waldron Cowdin.[2]

The older Robert Bacon (1860–1919) was a Harvard classmate of Theodore Roosevelt, graduating in 1880. He was a successful banker for two decades, first in Chicago and later in New York. Eventually he became a partner and second-in-command of J. P. Morgan and Company, resigning the latter position in 1903. In 1905 President Theodore Roosevelt named him assistant secretary of state (roughly equivalent to today's deputy

Robert Low Bacon rented the house at 1801 F Street from 1923 to 1925. He was reelected and owned it from 1925 to 1938. Like his father, an ambassador to France, he pursued a life in public service as a representative from New York. [C. E. Anderson, DACOR Bacon House Foundation Collection]

secretary), and in 1909 he succeeded Elihu Root as secretary of state for the final two month's of Roosevelt's presidency. From December 31, 1909, to April 19, 1912, Bacon was U.S. ambassador to France under President William Howard Taft. During World War I he served in France on the staff of General John J. Pershing, commander in chief of the American forces in Europe. After the war he was made a member of Harvard's Board of Overseers and a Fellow of the Harvard College Corporation.[3]

The elder Robert Bacon's life indicates that he was a cultured and talented gentleman. As one story illustrates, he was also a lucky man. When Bacon resigned his ambassadorship he made the customary arrangements to leave France before his replacement's arrival. However, a short time before his scheduled farewell, he received from Ambassador-designate Myron T. Herrick a request that he remain at post long enough to talk over various foreign policy matters. He courteously agreed to do so and canceled his sailing on the fateful maiden voyage of the *Titanic,* which sank after hitting an iceberg on April 14, 1912. In the aftermath of this tragedy, Ambassador Herrick wrote to Bacon on April 22, 1912, saying: "Of course you know that I've always thought you a most desirable citizen and have always admired Mrs. Bacon. It has not been my good fortune to know your daughter, but the vivid picture in my mind of you all on board the fated *Titanic* . . . has affected me more than I can tell you. . . . Had fate decreed you and your lovely family to have sailed out on the *Titanic,* France would have held no happiness for us."[4]

Martha Waldron Cowdin Bacon, the wife of Ambassador Bacon and mother of the future congressman, was a New Englander by birth who grew up in New York. Her grandfather, Thomas Cowdin, was a captain in the American army during the Revolution and a member of the Massachusetts legislature. Her father, Elliot C. Cowdin, was active in the nineteenth-century silk business and a strong supporter of the Union cause during the Civil War. When Cowdin died in 1880, General William Tecumseh Sherman said of him, "I can recall no more ardent, enthusiastic, and generous patriot."[5]

Born in 1884, Robert Low Bacon was graduated from Harvard in 1907 and earned a law degree there in 1910. Following graduation from law school, he worked for the U.S. Treasury Department for one year and then entered the banking business in New York. His marriage in 1913 to the wealthy, beautiful, and well-connected Virginia Murray was a highlight of the New York social season, uniting two equally prominent and

John Murray, fourth earl of Dunmore, was an ancestor of Virginia Bacon. This portrait is a copy by Winifred Gordon of the original by John Russell in 1765. [C. E. Anderson, DACOR Bacon House Foundation Collection]

wealthy families. In 1915 Bacon joined the New York National Guard, served with the U.S. Army from 1917 to 1919, and remained in the U.S. Army Officer Reserve Corps the rest of his life. A staunch Republican, he served in the House of Representatives for eight terms beginning in 1923. He died in office at the age fifty-four in 1938 and was buried in Arlington National Cemetery.[6]

Representative Bacon's signature piece of legislation was the Davis-Bacon Act of 1931. Controversial then and now, this legislation required contractors to pay "prevailing wages" established by the U.S. Department of Labor to each category of laborer working on individual federal construction projects. Unable to conduct the thousands of surveys that would have been required to comply with the letter of the act, the Department of Labor endeavored to fulfill the spirit of the act by certifying in many situations that existing union wages would be considered the prevailing wage. This practice effectively doubled the wage scale for most categories of workers on federal construction projects, as compared with the wage scales for equivalent workers engaged on nonfederal construction projects. In 1995 the Institute for Justice filed a lawsuit, as yet unsettled, asking that the legislation be declared unconstitutional as a violation of the Fifth Amendment guarantee of equal protection of the law.[7]

Virginia Murray was born in New York City on September 6, 1890, the first member of the Murray clan born in America after the onset of the American Revolution. In 1769 George II of England had appointed her paternal great-great-grandfather, Lord John Murray (1730–1809), fourth earl of Dunmore and a descendant of the House of Stuart, "His Majesty's Lieutenant, Vice Admiral, and Governour-General of the Colony and Dominion of New York."[8] In 1771 George III reassigned him to Williamsburg to discharge the same responsibilities in the colony and dominion of Virginia.

The first American-born Virginia Murray was a daughter of Lord

Murray and his wife, Lady Charlotte Stewart (1740–1810). Born in Williamsburg on December 8, 1774, she was named Virginia at the request of the Virginia Assembly, which expressed its pleasure at her birth by passing a provision that the child, upon coming of age, would receive £100,000. Regrettably for her, the colonies shortly thereafter signaled their desire to sever political connections with Great Britain. With the winds of independence sweeping the colonies, Lord Murray was obliged to flee the Governor's Palace on June 8, 1775. He, his wife, and four resident children (his five oldest children were in England) took refuge on the British man-of-war *Fowey* and returned to England. He revisited America briefly in 1787 after being named governor of the Bahamas, where he served until 1796.[9]

Virginia Murray, daughter of John Murray and Lady Charlotte Murray, was born in Williamsburg, Virginia in 1774. She was the first member of the Murray family to be named Virginia. [Frick Art Reference Library]

Virginia was only six months old when she was taken to England by her fleeing parents. Years later, after her father died, she wrote to Thomas Jefferson, thinking him to be governor of Virginia rather than president of the United States, begging that the £100,000 be paid. Jefferson sent the letter to James Madison, then governor of Virginia, who referred it to the Virginia legislature, which after consultation rejected her appeal. The colony of Virginia was also the inspiration for naming one of Governor Murray's grandsons Virginius. *Debrett's Peerage* shows that at least one other male and one other female of the family were given these same names in later generations.[10]

During the early decades of the next century, two other Murray family members visited the United States. The first was Lord Murray's grandson Augustus Frederick d'Este (1794–1848), a child of the morganatic marriage of Augusta Murray, the Murrays' daughter, to Prince Augustus Frederick, youngest son of King George III. (See page 134 for the complete story.) As a twenty-year-old lieutenant in the Seventh Royal Fusiliers, d'Este was sent to America as part of the seventy-five-hundred-man British army dispatched to press Great Britain's interests in the War of 1812. Sailing into the Gulf of Mexico late in December 1814, the British troops disembarked several miles below New Orleans. As aide-de-camp to Sir John Lambert, Lieutenant d'Este helped organize the invading forces, whose objective was to capture the city considered the key to controlling the Mississippi Valley.

On January 8, 1815, despite the signing on December 24, 1814, of the Treaty of Ghent, which ended the war, General Edward Pakenham ordered an all-out attack on a hastily assembled American army of six thousand men under the command of General Andrew Jackson. The fighting lasted less than thirty minutes. With almost three hundred British soldiers killed, including General Pakenham and most of the senior officers, and another seventeen hundred wounded (Jackson's losses were thirteen killed and sixty wounded), the British force, including d'Este, retreated across swamps to their waiting armada of fifty warships and sailed for England.[11]

The second family member to visit was Virginia Bacon's great-uncle, Charles Augustus Murray (1806–96), the son of George Murray, fifth earl of Dunmore. During the 1830s Charles traveled extensively in various parts of the world. Two of those years, beginning when he was twenty-eight, were spent exploring Canada and much of the United States east of the Mississippi River. Traveling at a leisurely pace and as transportation became available, he visited most of the country's major cities and dozens of small towns along the principal rivers. His itinerary included Williamsburg, Virginia, where he relived some of the experiences of his grandfather, Lord John Murray, the last British governor of Virginia.

While visiting Fort Leavenworth, Kansas, then the country's westernmost army post, Charles traveled on horseback into the Plains and lived with the Pawnee tribe for two months. In New Orleans he visited the battlefield where two decades earlier Jackson's forces had routed the British in the final battle of the War of 1812.

Once home, Charles prepared a detailed account of his world travels. Dedicated to Queen Victoria, volume three is devoted to his North American exploits. (The DACOR Bacon House Foundation has a copy of this volume.) Later in life, as the Right Honorable Sir Charles Augustus Murray, P.C., K.C.B., he was master of the household and extra groom in waiting to Queen Victoria and her diplomatic envoy to several European courts.[12]

Virginia Bacon's paternal great-grandfather, Alexander Murray (1764–1842), was the second son of Lady Charlotte and Lord John Murray and husband of Deborah (née Hunt) Murray. Alexander and Deborah's son Virginius Murray (1817–61) was Virginia Bacon's grandfather. Her father, Henry Alexander Murray (1857–1934), was one of the six sons of Virginius and Elizabeth (née Poitiers) Murray.[13]

The Murrays of Scotland were described rather glowingly by Charles Augustus Murray, Virginia Bacon's great-uncle, in his nineteenth-century journals:

> Some families are distinguished by their exploits in war, and some are enrolled in the pages of history for their abilities in peace; but none have shone more than the Murrays, whether we consider their general character for loyalty and bravery, their immense possessions, even in the tenth and eleventh centuries, and their alliances with almost every great house in Scotland.

The surname Murray is one of the most ancient in Scottish records and is supposed to be derived from the Moravii, who came from Germany and performed many signal services in favor of King Corbred I against the Romans; others are of the opinion that it originated in the county of Moray, where the family had large possessions at a very early period.[14]

The Murray family, including Virginia Bacon's direct line of ancestors and descendants, is extensively covered in *Burke's Peerage* and *Debrett's Peerage*. The earl of Dunmore's direct line of succession continues unbroken to this day. The eleventh earl was Kenneth Randolph Murray, the retired postmaster of Gravelly Beach, Tasmania, who succeeded to the title in 1981 and died in 1995. His son, Malcolm Kenneth Murray, born in 1946, inherited the title and is the twelfth earl of Dunmore.[15]

Virginia Bacon's earliest known maternal ancestor in the New World was James Babcock. Born in Essex, England, in 1612, he came to America in 1642. Through his second son, John, born in 1644, and his grandson James, born in 1664, the line to Virginia Bacon then ran through her great-great-great-great-grandfather, Joshua Babcock (1707–83). Distinguished in both his public and professional life, Joshua was a physician, chief justice of the colony of Rhode Island, a member of the Rhode Island Assembly, and the owner of a six-thousand-acre farm. Like other members of his family, he was a staunch patriot during the Revolution. His marriage to Hannah Stanton (1714–78) united two of the most prominent families among the early New England settlers. Of their several children, Henry, born in Westerly, Rhode Island, in 1736, was Virginia Bacon's great-great-great-grandfather.[16]

Graduating from Harvard at the top of his class at the age of sixteen,

Colonel Henry Babcock, Virginia Bacon's maternal great-great-great-grandfather, was born in 1736 to Joshua Babcock and Hannah Stanton Babcock. He was commander of the Continental forces of Rhode Island and fought in the Revolutionary War under the command of General George Washington. The portrait was painted by Otto Merkel in 1900 after the 1760s original by Joseph Blackburn. [Frick Art Reference Library]

Henry (called Harry) Babcock fought as a captain of infantry in the French and Indian War. For his bravery in capturing Baron Dieskau, the French commander at the battle of Lake George, he was promoted to major and was a colonel by the age of twenty-one. At the onset of the Revolution Harry was appointed commander of the Continental forces of Rhode Island, which fought courageously under General George Washington's command. After the war he settled in Stonington, Connecticut, where he practiced law and married Mary Stanton, a member of his mother's family. Their son, Paul, Virginia Bacon's great-great-grandfather, was born in 1768. Also inclined to the military, Paul rose to the rank of major but mostly followed the family tradition of mixing public service with farming.[17]

Of the several children of Paul Babcock and his wife, Nancy Bell, one, Benjamin Franklin Babcock (1790–1829), was named after the renowned patriot, who frequently stayed with the Babcocks when traveling in the area. One family tale recounts how, during one of his visits, Franklin installed lightning rods on the Babcock house.[18] In 1813 Benjamin married Maria Eells (1790–1852). Their fifth child, Samuel Denison Babcock (1822–1902), was Virginia Bacon's maternal grandfather.

A prominent New Yorker and eminent financier, Samuel was a participant in the banking firms of Babcock Brothers and Company of New York and the Central Trust of New York and a founder and first president of the Guaranty Trust of New York. He was also president of both the New York, New Haven, and Hartford Railroad and the International Bell Telephone Company, as well as a director of a score of other major corporations, including several railroads. For seven years he headed the New York Chamber of Commerce. In 1846 Samuel Babcock married Elizabeth Crary Franklin (1828–81). In 1889 one of their seven daughters, Fannie Morris Babcock (1856–1940), married Henry Alexander Murray.[19]

Although Henry Alexander Murray descended from the fourth earl of

Dunmore, he grew up in modest circumstances as the fourth of the six sons of Virginius Murray, an army officer in Her Majesty's service. Virginius's last assignment, with the rank of captain, was as aide-de-camp to the commander in chief of British forces in Canada. In 1849 he elected to sell his commission and retire. For the next nine years he held an appointment as commissioner of gold fields and police magistrate in the colony of Victoria, Australia, until his untimely death in 1861, when Henry was just four. His widow returned with her six sons to England, where, thanks to the Murray family prestige and influence, young Henry was admitted to the highly regarded Christ's Hospital charity school. Although he did well in his studies, he cut short his education when his mother died and while still in his teens emigrated to Canada to start a new life.

When after a year he failed to turn up any challenging opportunities in Toronto, he moved on to New York and found employment in a securities firm. After ten years of slow but steady progress in his career, his fortunes took a sharp upward turn when he met and won the heart of Fannie Morris Babcock and the favor of the wealthy and socially prominent Babcock family. After marrying Fannie in 1889, and with the help of his influential father-in-law, Murray quickly rose to prominence in New York City's financial and social circles. For the remainder of their lives, Henry and Fannie would enjoy a patrician lifestyle marked by luxury and security. They had three children, Virginia, Henry Jr., and Cecil.[20] The eldest, Virginia, born in 1890, would become Mrs. Robert Low Bacon.

The elder of Virginia's brothers, Henry Alexander Murray Jr. (1893–1988), attended Groton, where during his third term he roomed with the future secretary of state Dean Acheson. A graduate of Harvard University in 1915 and Columbia College of Physicians and Surgeons in 1919, Henry added a master's degree in biology from Columbia and a Ph.D. from Cambridge University before completing his medical internship. He devoted most of his adult life to teaching and research in psychology at Harvard. Virginia's younger brother, Cecil Dunmore Murray, born in 1897, followed his brother Henry to Groton, Harvard (1919), and the Columbia College of Physicians and Surgeons (1923). During World War I he was a U.S. Navy pilot in Europe and earned the Navy Cross for conspicuous heroism. His career in the field of psychology was cut short by his death in 1935 of Hodgkin's disease.[21]

Growing up in New York City, Virginia Murray attended the prestigious

Virginia Murray Bacon lived at 1801 F Street with her husband, Representative Robert Low Bacon of New York, beginning in 1923, when they first rented the house. They purchased the house two years later and after his death in 1938 she remained as owner until her death in 1980. [DACOR Bacon House Foundation Collection]

The north drawing room, seen about 1930, is linked to the south drawing room, dining room, and gallery in a manner that invites formal entertaining. [DACOR Bacon House Foundation Collection]

Johanna Davidge School, where one of her classmates was Ethel Roosevelt, the daughter of the soon-to-be-president Theodore Roosevelt. As a result of this connection, she was often Ethel's house guest at the White House. In later years, when prodded, Virginia Bacon would relate how her train to Washington would be met at the station by uniformed White House staff members, who would drive her to the executive mansion in a horse-drawn landau.

These fun-filled visits sometimes included water fights in the second-floor corridor using pitchers of water as ammunition, a favorite form of entertainment. Also popular, although frowned on, was the practice of "belly wafting" down the mansion's state staircase on tin trays. The trick, Virginia Bacon would explain, was to make the trays spin in a circle at a speed sufficient to navigate the hairpin turns without bumping into the walls or colliding with the children in front of or behind you. The Roosevelt boys—Teddy Jr., Kermit, Archibald, and Quentin—were the experts in this reckless game. On Sunday mornings Virginia often went horseback riding with President Roosevelt and his family.

In 1910, while in London with her parents, Virginia attended the funeral of Edward VII and had a reunion with the Roosevelt family, who were visiting England at the same time. In 1911 she was presented to George V and Queen Mary at the Royal Court at Holyrood Palace, Edinburgh.

In the decade following their marriage on April 14, 1913, the Bacons made their home in New York, interrupted by World War I. As a member of the National Guard, Robert Bacon was called to duty at military posts in New York, Texas, Georgia, South Carolina, Washington, D.C., and Oklahoma. His wife accompanied him on some of these assignments. Returning to New York after the armistice, they made their home at Arlough, a country estate in Westbury, Long Island, designed by John Russell Pope. Summers found them at Mid River Farm in the Thousand Islands on the St. Lawrence River. Early in 1923, following Bacon's election to the U.S. House of Representatives, the Bacons came to Washington, D.C., and took up residence at the 1801 F Street house.[22]

Because of her upbringing, her wealth, and her husband's position, Virginia Bacon rapidly became one of the grandes dames of Washington, a position she maintained after the congressman's death in 1938. Together with Mildred Bliss and Marie Beale, she was one of the trio known familiarly as the "three Bs."[23] All patrons of the arts, they were much admired for their hospitality and generosity. Virginia Bacon entertained often and with great panache, and political and social leaders frequently gathered at the F Street house for lively discussions and cultural events. Several sitting presidents, including Dwight Eisenhower and Richard Nixon, as well as two future presidents, George Bush and Gerald Ford, were her guests. The musicians Arthur Rubinstein and Eugene Ormandy often stayed with her when they performed in Washington.[24]

An interesting and oft-repeated tale is told about Rubinstein. In 1929 Virginia Bacon purchased a Steinway grand piano, still in the north drawing room. It is a fine instrument that Rubinstein, it is said, helped her select. It is certain that the "prince of pianists" played the instrument on those occasions when he and his wife, Nela, were Virginia Bacon's house guests. On such visits, longtime friends recall, Rubinstein sometimes played brief after-dinner private concerts for his hostess and her guests.

In his memoirs, *My Many Years,* Rubinstein wrote:

My appearances in Washington were very special. It is the only place in the world where I welcomed the hospitality of a private home. Virginia Bacon was the kind of hostess who had the gift of making you feel really free in her home. It is true that her house was considered a historic mansion with a lovely garden and was quite near Constitution Hall, where I used to play. She lived alone, in the luxury of the good old days. Over the years she considered us family. She loved to travel with us and had accompanied me with Nela, Eva, and Paul on a tour to South America which took us to Brazil, Argentina, Chile, and Peru. She came with us to Greece, to Poland and Paris. In Washington itself she gave parties after every concert of mine. A woman of extraordinary vigor, she would never miss any social gathering; lunch, dinner, supper, or ball, one could always count on her presence and she keeps it up until this hour as I write. [Rubinstein's memoirs were published in 1980, the year of Virginia Bacon's death.][25]

Virginia Bacon was a staunch supporter of various organizations concerned with international relations, among them the World Affairs Council. Of these council meetings, Barbara Bush, the former First Lady, in her book *Barbara Bush: A Memoir,* wrote: "Once a month . . . I attended the Washington World Affairs Council luncheon where Mrs. Virginia Bacon, widow of a New York congressman and an old grande dame, invited fascinating speakers to tell us about the world. They were very informative luncheons, but the thing I remember most was the fact that Mrs. Bacon put her head back and slept soundly and noisily through every speech. It was amusing to watch the speaker when he or she realized that Mrs. Bacon was asleep and then tried to act like it didn't matter."[26]

Like her husband, Virginia Bacon was active in Republican Party affairs and was both a state and a national convention delegate. In 1955 President Dwight D. Eisenhower appointed her, with the personal rank of ambassador, to be his representative at the Silver Jubilee of Emperor Haile Selassie, and in 1956 he accorded her the same honor at the coronation of King Mahendra of Nepal. Eisenhower also named her to the Advisory Committee on the Arts for the National Cultural Center. She was for many years a member of the Adelphi University Board of Trustees and of several committees supporting opera companies and symphony orchestras in New York, Philadelphia, and Washington. For her relief work in World War II, she was awarded the Order of the British Empire, the French Legion of Honor, the White Rose of Finland, and Italy's Stella della-Solidarieta.[27]

Robert and Virginia Bacon had three daughters. Alexandra, who was

In the north drawing room above the fireplace hangs an English giltwood mirror from about 1760. Its dramatic curves complement the Bacons' other antique and oriental furnishings. [DACOR Bacon House Foundation Collection]

born in 1914, died in 1935. Virginia, born in 1916, married Byron Thomas. Martha, born in 1918, first married Creighton Churchill and later James L. Farley; she died in 1990.

On buying the house in 1925, the Bacons freshened it by repainting it both outside and inside, repapering various rooms, and remodeling the top floor to create a suite of ten rooms with two full baths and one half bath. They furnished the house with an assemblage of furniture, paintings, and art objects brought from their New York residence or acquired from the estates of their parents. The circa 1760 large, carved giltwood overmantel mirror in the main drawing room was purchased in London in 1906 by Alice Thaw. It still dominates that room and is purported to

The wrought-iron New Orleans–style porch, designed by Louis A. Simons, was added in 1949 to cover the open forecourt that linked the mansion to the carriage house. [DACOR Bacon House Foundation Collection]

be the work of the eighteenth-century craftsman Thomas Johnson. On selling the house to the Bacons, Alice Thaw (by then Alice Whitney) sold the mirror in a separate transaction because, as she wrote in a personal letter to Virginia Bacon, "I have no place for it in our Connecticut house." The international ambiance of the house was created in part by the Bacons' extensive collection of oriental art, part of which was inherited, part purchased during their congressional travels in the Far East, and part acquired before their marriage during a buying spree that followed Virginia Murray's good fortune in winning $3,676 in the Peking Sweepstakes.[28]

To connect the carriage house to the main house, Virginia Bacon in 1949 added a New Orleans–style porch designed by Louis A. Simon. At the same time the carriage house was remodeled to provide improved quarters for the chauffeur and an enlarged laundry facility.[29]

The west garden, enclosed by a red brick wall, was an important element in the Bacons' lifestyle. Heavily shrubbed, the garden had an

English country air, a feeling heightened by the ivy that almost totally covered the house. The lower third of the garden, the principal entertainment area, was covered in brick laid in a herringbone pattern, while the rest of the garden was mostly grass. Meandering brick footpaths circled the perimeters, with various flower beds in which Virginia Bacon grew her favorite roses. Along the south wall an extended wrought-iron bar served as support for lush wisteria vines. The southwest corner had a modest pergola that stood over a nineteenth-century marble table. Viewed from any vantage point, the sylvan garden offered contrasts in scale, shapes, texture, and color.

It was Virginia Bacon who planted the garden's majestic trees. In 1958, a *Washington Post* article relates, she purchased a thirty-five-foot-tall oak tree and, to avoid trying up traffic, had it moved to her home during the night from Silver Spring, Maryland. The next day three cranes were required to lift the fifteen-ton tree over the wall. Now ten feet in girth and sixty feet tall, the tree shades much of the garden. A week after the tree was put in place, Virginia Bacon welcomed 350 guests to a garden party honoring Ambassador and Mrs. Robert Woods Bliss. In 1964, to further shelter the garden and to gain an added measure of privacy, she planted nine *Magnolia grandiflora* trees that hug the north and west boundaries and obscure the two office buildings that abut the garden on those sides.

An array of wrought-iron furniture and a few fanciful accessories gave the garden a comfortable look that made it a welcoming refuge, especially during the trying years of World War II, when Virginia Bacon hosted daily, open-house buffet luncheons. Military friends, statesmen, and civic leaders were invited to drop by, unannounced, to enjoy a brief respite from their wartime duties. Generally, one or two dozen friends gathered there each day. On those occasions when the weather was fine, guests sat in the garden at two turn-of-the-century French tables, each with four matching arm chairs. These pieces had been purchased in Paris in 1909 by Robert Bacon Sr. (Representative Bacon's father), when he was U.S. ambassador to France. Brought to America in 1912, the tables and chairs graced the garden at Ambassador Bacon's Long Island estate for several years. In the mid-1920s Representative Bacon brought this furniture to Washington, along with several English pieces, including two nineteenth-century griffin-legged, laurel-leaf settees and a small, round, pierced-top table. The remainder of the garden's wrought-iron furniture—several tables and sixteen matching chairs—was added during the 1940s and 1950s.[30]

CHAPTER EIGHT

TWO GREAT TRADITIONS MERGE

1975–1986

One gathers a true appreciation for the diversity of furniture and furnishings that the Bacons exhibited during their residence with this view of the south drawing room. [DACOR Bacon House Foundation Collection]

IN THE MID-1960S, as she approached her seventy-fifth birthday, Virginia Bacon grew increasingly concerned about the future of her home. Preservation of the house for future generations was, in her view, a clear obligation. She would thereby follow the precedents set by Ambassador and Mrs. Robert Woods Bliss, who left their Georgetown estate, Dumbarton Oaks, to Harvard University, and by Marie Beale, who left her Lafayette Square home, Decatur House, to the National Trust for Historic Preservation. Motivating Virginia Bacon was the realization that despite several renovations, her home retained much of its original scale and craftsmanship and was one of the last remaining architecturally prized, early-nineteenth-century homes in the rapidly developing commercial area near the White House. Moreover, she was keenly aware that the house was a microcosm of a century and a half of Washington's cultural and social history, and she intended to preserve that history.

Her initial thought was to transfer the house to the National Trust, which was interested in acquiring it for the organization's national headquarters. This idea appealed to her, as she was not interested in having the house "simply be a museum or historic site." Instead, she preferred that it "enjoy a lively existence consistent with the interests and connections of its occupants through the years, and be characterized by dignity, taste, and intelligence." Before this transfer could be completed, however, the plan was dropped because of altered National Trust considerations.[1]

In 1964, when the transfer was pending, the National Trust acquired the front door, portico, and palladian windows of Louise du Pont Crowninshield's Marblehead, Massachusetts, home, then being demolished. The Trust did so in the belief that this architectural ensemble was the original entrance installed on the 1801 F Street house in 1825 by Tench Ringgold.[2] There is no firm evidence to support the claim, but if it was the original structure, it had no doubt been changed in the 1860s by the Carroll family. The Crowninshield pieces remain stored at Oatlands, a National Trust property in northern Virginia, pending a decision on how best to use them. One possibility would be to incorporate the door into a future annex that may be built in the northwest corner of the garden at DACOR Bacon House.

In 1970 Mark O. Hatfield, Oregon's Republican senator and an old family friend, became aware of Virginia Bacon's efforts to preserve the house. Believing that her interests and those of the American people could be mutually served, he introduced legislation in the Senate proposing that the U.S. government accept and maintain Bacon House as the official residence of a high government official to be designated by the president. Ever mindful of the long association between 1801 F Street and both the Supreme Court and the Diplomatic and Consular Services, Virginia Bacon suggested that either the sitting chief justice of the United States or the secretary of state would be a logical choice. Despite its appeal, the idea was dropped because of the government's reluctance to open the door to a policy of providing housing for senior officials other than the president and vice president.[3]

Disappointed that Senator Hatfield's effort had failed, Virginia Bacon tried a different tack to achieve a similar objective. In August 1971 she had a proposal prepared to establish the Virginia and Robert Low Bacon Foundation. Its purpose was to operate Bacon House as a guest facility for foreign dignitaries visiting the United States as official guests of the chief justice or the secretary of state. The inspiration for this idea was the president's guest house, the Blair-Lee mansion on Pennsylvania Avenue, but the proposal was abandoned for lack of support.[4]

At another point, negotiations were entered into with the John F. Kennedy Center for the Performing Arts to make Bacon House a guest facility for the center's most important visiting artists. Also considered were suggestions that Bacon House become the Washington counterpart of the New York–based Council on Foreign Relations or the headquarters for the Aspen Institute. The latter organization's insistence on holding title to the property and on having its name imposed on the house was reason enough for Virginia Bacon to quash the idea. Similarly, she vetoed a suggestion that the house be used by the Smithsonian Institution because of its insistence on holding title to the property.[5]

Convinced that the preservation of her historic house could best be achieved by creating her own tax-exempt entity to own and operate it, Virginia Bacon elected in 1975 to establish the Bacon House Foundation. In her words, it would be "dedicated in memory of my late husband, U.S. Representative Robert Low Bacon, and be an informal meeting place where statesmen and those who, like him, devote their lives to civic service, can get together and exchange views on world problems."[6] Acting favorably on her petition, the District of Columbia Recorder of Deeds issued a certificate, dated June 4, 1975, attesting to the incorporation of Bacon House as a nonprofit corporation pursuant to the provisions of the District of Columbia Non-Profit Corporation Act.

Two years earlier, in 1973, Virginia Bacon had signaled her projected course of action by requesting that Bacon House be listed in the National Register of Historic Places. Acknowledging that the house was of historical importance, the National Register promptly approved the listing, effective July 26, 1973.[7]

As an integral part of her action to establish the new foundation, Virginia Bacon created an eleven-person board of directors whose members, all friends of many years, were distinguished statesmen, civic leaders, scholars, or preservationists. In addition to herself, the board included Charles R. Norbert, John S. Thatcher, Richard H. Howland, George C. McGhee, Lucius D. Battle, Herman C. Phleger, Samuel E. Belk III, Caroline Simmons, Lisa Sergio, and H. Chapman Rose. As circumstances dictated, other friends were consulted and new board members added, among them Robert G. Cleveland, William N. Cafritz, J. Robert McNaughton, Jacob D. Beam, Evangeline and David K. E. Bruce, Marion Charles, Randolph A. Kidder, Gerson Nordlinger Jr., Senator Hugh Scott, Diana Sartoris, William J. Casey, Justice Potter Stewart, Philip W. Bonsal, James H. Billington, Chester L. Cooper, Martha Farley, and Charles S. Whitehouse.[8]

During 1977 three key administrative matters were favorably resolved.

A view into the south drawing room during the Bacon era reveals the chandelier installed in the 1860s and the black marble mantel added in 1911. [DACOR Bacon House Foundation Collection]

First, the Bacon House Foundation gained accreditation as a tax-exempt organization. On May 24, 1977, the Internal Revenue Service granted temporary "private foundation" status under section 501(c)(3) of the code. This status was retroactive to June 4, 1975, and ran through December 31, 1980. After reviewing the foundation's activities during the first five years, the Internal Revenue Service, on October 29, 1981, granted permanent tax-exempt status.

Next, on June 4, 1977, the Bacon House Foundation and the government of the District of Columbia entered into a Historic Preservation Covenant. Under its terms the District granted the foundation a real property tax reduction for twenty years (fiscal years 1977 through 1997). In return, the foundation agreed to maintain the historical, aesthetic, and cultural character and condition of the house throughout the tax abatement period.[9]

Finally, on July 20, 1977, Virginia Bacon deeded "forever" to the

National Trust for Historic Preservation an "easement of scenic, open space, and architectural facade" on the house, thus ensuring that the footprint of the existing structure and its exterior architectural features would never be changed.[10]

With these steps taken, Virginia Bacon and the foundation's board of directors, operating primarily through an executive committee headed by the acting president Lucius D. Battle, turned their attention to financing and shaping the organization's educational programs. One early possibility for long-term financing was to lease two adjoining Bacon-owned lots, 1811 and 1813 F Street, to a builder who would construct an office building. Such use of the property would produce income through rentals and provide space for the foundation's larger conference activities. Virginia Bacon pursued this idea to the point of also purchasing the lots at 1815 and 1817 F Street from the Marshburn estate on April 8, 1974. This action gave her control of the entire north side of F Street between 18th and 19th Streets, except for the corner lot at 19th Street, site of the Town House Apartments. On completing the purchase, she obtained a permit to raze the circa 1839 red brick house and the circa 1871 green stone houses that occupied these sites—much to the consternation of preservation groups.

Now in control of almost the entire half block, Virginia Bacon engaged the architectural firm of Sasaki Associates of Watertown, Massachusetts, to devise a "design approach" for the proposed office building. Mindful of her insistence that the new structure be architecturally harmonious with Bacon House, Sasaki proposed a red brick building, seven stories high at the point farthest from Bacon House, then downsized in step fashion to three stories where it abutted the Bacon House garden. Oliver T. Carr, a well-known Washington developer, expressed interest in the project and reached an informal agreement-in-principle with Virginia Bacon to construct the contemplated building.[11]

As plans for the project fell into place, Virginia Bacon was approached on a quite different proposition. Inter-American Properties, seeking a site for a new office building for the Organization of American States (OAS), proposed purchasing her adjoining properties. After careful consideration she agreed to sell the four vacant lots for $2.35 million. In a separate transaction, Inter-American Properties purchased the adjoining Town House Apartment complex. The funds derived from this sale enabled Virginia Bacon to establish for the Bacon House Foundation an endowment of $1.2 million, thus putting in place one of the building blocks for the foundation's long-range financial stability.

A condition of the sale was an agreement that the OAS building would be designed so that it would not overwhelm her historic house or its walled garden. The solution was to have the east end of the proposed office building curve inward to form an open space for a landscaped sunken garden that would complement the adjacent Bacon House garden. Construction on the OAS building was completed in July 1979.[12]

For the foundation's educational programs the board studied many existing organizations, seeking an ideal model. One attractive possibility was that of Ditchley House in England. In pursuit of this idea Virginia Bacon, the British ambassador, and the foundation's board of directors hosted a reception at Bacon House on May 5, 1976. It was the first major event conducted in the name of the new foundation. The guests of honor were Sir David Wills, chairman of the Ditchley Council, and Sir Michael Stewart, director of the Ditchley Foundation. Invited to attend were more than one hundred U.S. senators and representatives who had participated in Ditchley seminars, as well as a "who's who" of professional foreign policy officials, international organization representatives, resident diplomats, and civic and cultural leaders. Five months later on October 8, 1976, Virginia Bacon and the board of directors, in conjunction with the American Ditchley Foundation, hosted a second reception. Although the two organizations cooperated with each other, they did not establish a formal relationship.

The Bacon House Foundation also explored other organizations as models, including the World Affairs Councils of Philadelphia and Northern California and the New York Council on Foreign Relations. From its study of such organizations the foundation quickly realized that such programs could be conducted more easily and at higher levels in the nation's capital, thanks to its colony of foreign diplomats and international organization representatives and its steady flow of international visitors. The Bacon House Foundation thus began to sponsor a spate of educational foreign affairs programs. Included were seminars and discussions on China, Lebanon, the Middle East, Africa, U.S.–U.S.S.R. relations, Russian law, and a European Parliamentary Group meeting.[13]

By the late 1970s the board of directors realized that Virginia Bacon's $1.2 million endowment, while adequate to generate the funds needed to maintain the residence as a setting for the foundation's endeavors, was not sufficient to renovate the house, hire a staff, and pay the expenses of organizing and conducting an array of educational endeavors. The realistic solution was to find a compatible organization willing to join forces with Bacon House Foundation, not only to support its educational programs but also to help fund the renovation of the house. Suitable candidates included the Council on Foreign Relations, Stanley Foundation, German Marshall Fund, and Johns Hopkins Evergreen House. The directors decided, however, that the organizations best matching the character, purposes, and style of the Bacon House Foundation were DACOR (Diplomatic and Consular Officers, Retired) and its tax-exempt DACOR Educational and Welfare Foundation. Virginia Bacon supported this idea, confident that the resulting center would foster international understanding.[14]

At this juncture on February 24, 1980, Virginia Murray Bacon died at the age of eighty-nine and title to Bacon House passed to the Bacon House Foundation. To the foundation's board now fell the task of converting Bacon House from a private residence into an educational center. As a first step the board invited several prominent architects to submit proposals for renovating the house. After careful consideration, J. L. Sibley Jennings, AIA, was engaged on March 22, 1982, to develop a phased architectural renovation.

The carriage house, all agreed, had to be renovated first. The exterior, protected by the National Trust easement, was to be left unchanged. A completely refurbished interior, however, would provide twenty-five hundred square feet of space. It could then accommodate the offices of the Bacon House Foundation as well as those of other suitable nonprofit organizations, whose rental fees would provide needed operating income. The Joint Committee on Landmarks, the Commission of Fine Arts, and the District of Columbia government readily approved the project, and a construction permit was granted on December 8, 1982. Renovation began in March 1983 with the carriage house costs projected at $271,000, within an overall Bacon House budget of $1.1 million.[15]

Nine months later the carriage house renovation was completed, having created six comfortable offices, three on each floor. The largest, stretching almost the entire length of the ground floor, had three working levels. A staircase led to the second floor. Along the south side and accessible from the west garden was the stall room, so called because it retained two of the spoked dividers that in earlier years had created separate stalls for the horses. In the back, with access to the service yard, was a third office. On the second floor, in addition to three large offices, were two tiled bathrooms and a small kitchenette.

Visible from the 18th Street driveway, the original 1860s wooden hoist beam has remained in place, carefully preserved by the Bacon House Foundation in the 1983–84 renovation. For the outstanding restoration of the "mews," the American Institute of Architects on September 29, 1984, awarded the Bacon House Foundation a citation for "Achievement of Excellence in Historic Preservation and Architecture."[16]

The Bacon House Foundation established its headquarters in the stall room in January 1984, at which time the remainder of the space was rented to Arts International and the Japan-America Society of Washington, D.C. One year later, when Arts International moved its offices to New York, its space was taken over by the Japan-America Student Conference and the Institute for Puerto Rican Affairs. Late in 1993 when the Japan-America Society also moved, that space was leased to William W. Becker, an attorney, and to the public accountant firm Howard L. Carter and Associates. At the end of 1995 after the Institute for Puerto Rican Affairs closed its offices, DACOR reclaimed that space for use as an administrative support facility.[17]

Meanwhile, plans for the renovation of the main residence progressed. Jennings, the architect, developed a plan, tentatively approved by the board, to convert the two top floors of the house into office space for rental to nonprofit organizations and restore the two bottom floors to serve the Bacon House Foundation's needs. The final drawings for this phase of the project were ready in December 1983 but the foundation's financial situation posed a serious problem. To resolve it, the executive committee worked with local banks and approached such institutions as the Ford Foundation to obtain loans or grants to support the construction effort. The board also explored with the Organization of American States a proposal for joint cooperation on educational projects and with the OAS General Secretariat to provide full management and maintenance services for the house. Simultaneously, discussions were held with the Wilson Center, which proposed renting the office space and conducting, either as sponsor or cosponsor, a discussion group series on foreign affairs topics.[18]

Other interested groups came forward to explore the possibility of using the house under some mutually satisfactory arrangement. The Holiday Foundation wanted to acquire the entire house to use it as a National

The gallery, seen about 1930 from the dining room, featured a Dutch prelate's chair from the late seventeenth century and a trestle table from the nineteenth century. [DACOR Bacon House Foundation Collection]

Museum of Women in the Arts. The World Affairs Council asked for priority in renting the two top floors and offered full cooperation in cosponsoring a wide-ranging public education program. The Pan American Development Foundation and the Center for Latin American Studies of the Americas, possibly as part of the agreement under which the OAS General Secretariat would manage Bacon House, also expressed interest in locating their offices in the renovated mansion.[19]

While possibilities for new arrangements for Bacon House were under consideration, discussions between Bacon House Foundation and DACOR and the DACOR Educational and Welfare Foundation took on a growing sense of urgency. Joining forces, it was agreed, would serve the best interests of both organizations. Both had tax-exempt status under section 501 (c)(3) of the Internal Revenue Code, and both enjoyed certain tax advantages with the government of the District of Columbia. Not only would the merger give DACOR the larger quarters it sought, but DACOR's 2,300 members and its financial resources would ensure both the renovation of Bacon House and a continuing educational program in foreign affairs.

As prospects for the merger of the two foundations brightened, the Bacon House Foundation executive committee sought new architectural support, both to energize the renovation work already in progress and to plot the changes needed to meet the operational requirements of the new foundation to result from the proposed merger. To that end, the committee entered into a contract with the Washington architecture firm Archetype on December 20, 1984.

A specialist in restoring historic properties, Archetype quickly researched the evolution of the house from its construction in 1825 through the alterations and additions by four successive owners over the next 160 years. Despite the absence of some original source material, the findings were quite comprehensive and suggested fresh opportunities for desirable improvements. Archetype's findings highlighted sharp distinctions between those architectural features that had to be preserved at all cost and those elements that could be altered or even eliminated without sacrificing authenticity or endangering the historical character of the house's interiors.

Drawing on this history and emphasizing restoration and preservation rather than renovation and modernization, plans were crafted to create an elegant, functional setting in which to carry out the multifaceted educational programs and member-support activities of the soon-to-be DACOR Bacon House Foundation. At the same time the new plans took fully into account the preservation mandates of the several overseer organizations, in particular the Commission of Fine Arts and the National Trust for Historic Preservation.

Under the revised concept, the top floor was converted from office space to five bedrooms, each with a private bath. The third floor remained office space. On the second floor the entertainment rooms remained essentially unchanged, but a full-scale kitchen was added to facilitate the numerous luncheons, dinners, and receptions projected as part of future educational endeavors. The ground floor was altered to create the present meeting room and a library.[20]

While these changes were being plotted, advance assurances were sought and obtained from both the U.S. and District of Columbia governments that the foundation to be formed would enjoy the same nonprofit, tax-free status as the two predecessor organizations. With that legal matter favorably resolved, the Bacon House Foundation board of directors approved the "Articles of Merger" on April 23, 1985. The board of governors of Diplomatic and Consular Officers, Retired, and the board of trustees of the DACOR Educational and Welfare Foundation approved the document on April 25, 1985. On April 26, the formal merger agreement was signed by both parties, and on the same date the superintendent of corporations of the District of Columbia duly recorded the existence of the new entity—DACOR Bacon House Foundation—with title to 1801 F Street vested in the new organization.[21]

The members of the board of governors of DACOR and of the board of trustees of the DACOR Educational and Welfare Foundation who considered and voted to effect the merger were H. Gardiner Ainsworth, Milton Barall, Leland Barrows, Robert M. Beers, Elmer H. Bourgerie, H. Daniel Brewster, L. Dean Brown, William D. Calderhead, Robert W. Caldwell, Jacob Canter, Robert G. Cleveland, William B. Cobb Jr., William A. Crawford, Joseph F. Donelan Jr., Rose Fales, Richard Funkhouser,

Theodore J. Hadraba, Henry F. Hemmerich, Spencer M. King, LaRue R. Lutkins, James K. Penfield, Claude G. Ross, Walter J. Stoessel Jr., Jane Thompson, and Charles S. Whitehouse. The organization's officers at the time were Ben Hill Brown, president; William C. Trueheart, vice president; Joseph F. Donelan Jr., treasurer; William D. Calderhead, assistant treasurer; William B. Cobb, secretary; James B. Opsata, assistant secretary; and Allen B. Moreland, executive director. In addition, the executive committee consisted of the past president Horace G. Torbert Jr., Spencer M. King, Leland Barrows, and Elmer H. Bourgerie.[22]

On June 28, 1985, the District of Columbia government issued a permit to renovate DACOR Bacon House. Thus began a yearlong frenzy of renovation activity, supervised by the building committee, headed by William N. Cafritz, and spearheaded by the general contractor, Hercules and Company of Washington, D.C. A new office entrance emerged, as did a fireproof staircase, an elevator, a caretaker's efficiency apartment, and additional bathrooms. Old floors were reinforced and windows refitted. Along the way, new electrical and plumbing systems, a security system, an emergency lighting system, and a housewide telephone network were put in place. Meanwhile, a dedicated group of craftsmen, exercising great care, variously repaired, reinforced, stripped, patched, sanded, and, where necessary, replaced walls, floors, ceilings, moldings, and fireplaces.

While the restoration work was progressing, the decorating committee, headed by Rose Fales and assisted by the professional interior decorator Sherry Geyelin, planned how best to decorate the twenty-four rooms of the emerging DACOR Bacon House. In a most gracious act of generosity, Virginia Bacon, in addition to leaving her historic house to the Bacon House Foundation, also willed to it a collection of antique furnishings sufficient to furnish the principal entertainment rooms in a characteristically nineteenth-century manner. Added to this good fortune were the eclectic and valuable collection of antique furnishings, oriental art, books, and Foreign Service memorabilia DACOR had accumulated over four decades. From these two treasure troves the decorating committee selected, some weeks in advance of actually decorating the house, various items to be repaired, restored, refinished, or reupholstered. It chose new rugs and fabrics for everything from curtains to bedspreads and sorted and cleaned an array of accessories, including a superb collection of portraits and oriental art.

At the end of May 1986, when DACOR sold the structure housing its offices at 1718 H Street, N.W., for $1.5 million, the house committee,

The garden room, photographed about 1930, allows access to the garden via a small open porch added in 1896. On the walls are nineteenth-century engravings of prominent Americans (above and opposite). [DACOR Bacon House Foundation Collection]

headed by William D. Calderhead, packed the remainder of DACOR's furnishings, books, and memorabilia and moved them to 1801 F Street. At the same time the remainder of Virginia Bacon's effects were brought from storage. For the next two weeks a team of dedicated Dacorians worked tirelessly to put everything in place in the pristine rooms of the newly rechristened DACOR Bacon House.[23]

At the inaugural ceremony on May 23, 1986, the newly formed DACOR Bacon House Foundation was addressed by its president, Ben Hill Brown, who had been president of the former DACOR Educational and Welfare Foundation. Ambassador Brown told the gathering:

The merger of Bacon House Foundation and DACOR Educational and Welfare Foundation was a superb blending of two organizations striving to achieve common goals. Both organizations have eagerly accepted the merger as a challenge to expand our horizons, to be more creative in our thinking, and to be

more imaginative in planning programs which will enable us better and more completely to realize the noble objectives for which we were organized.[24]

Ambassador Lucius D. Battle, president of the former Bacon House Foundation and the first vice president of the newly formed DACOR Bacon House Foundation, also addressed the inaugural gathering, saying:

> Today we are merging two great traditions—the tradition of the Foreign Service of the United States . . . and the judicial, congressional, and cultural tradition of this house. Here statesmen, presidents, diplomats, and world leaders have come, have talked, have dealt with problems—even solved a few—and I am confident the house will in the future continue to play that international role.[25]

The guests of honor at the inaugural ceremony were Secretary of State George P. Shultz and his wife, Helena Shultz. Secretary Shultz told the assembled guests:

The goals of DACOR Bacon House Foundation and the goals of our country's diplomacy and the Department of State are basically the same. We want to protect and advance the interests and ideals of America. DACOR's members, whose experience and knowledge of diplomacy are without equal, are vital assets to American foreign policy. DACOR's founders understood the contribution that retired members of the Foreign Service could make, and they understood, too, that only such an institution as this could insure continuity from one generation to the next. America and all of [its] public servants will need you in the coming years, and we look forward to the continued well-being and vitality of DACOR and the programs that bear its name.[26]

A bronze plaque dated 1986 mounted at the F Street entrance was dedicated at the ceremony. It reads:

Given by Virginia Murray Bacon in memory of her husband, Representative Robert Low Bacon of New York, as a center to further international understanding. The building was restored for this purpose by DACOR Bacon House Foundation. This property is listed in the National Register of Historic Places and protected by an easement held by the National Trust for Historic Preservation.

On June 6, 1986, when DACOR resumed its members-only luncheon series, sixty people attended. This was followed by various DACOR Bacon House Foundation events. Thus began a new chapter of educational and cultural activity, which attracted more than a quarter of a million visitors in the first ten years.

On September 26, 1986, the American Institute of Architects, judging the overall restoration of the mansion to be truly outstanding, honored the DACOR Bacon House Foundation, the architect Archetype, and the general contractor Hercules and Company by presenting them each with a citation for "Excellence in Historic Preservation and Architecture."[27]

Once the DACOR Bacon House Foundation had established normal operations, it took long-planned steps to rent the third-floor space to compatible nonprofit organizations. The Consortium of Washington Universities, a new entity representing special educational interests of four area universities, initially rented the entire floor, opening its offices on July 1, 1987. Because the space was larger than needed, however, the consortium subleased two offices to the Christopher Columbus Quincentenary Jubilee Commission. One year later, quite unexpectedly, the consortium ceased operations. Meanwhile, the Columbus Commission had expanded its operations and staff and elected to rent the entire floor, effective July 1, 1988. The commission remained active through June 30, 1993.

At this juncture the DACOR Bacon House Foundation began to use the third floor for educational seminars, foreign affairs conferences, committee meetings, and various administrative purposes. The minor budgetary problems caused by the resulting loss of rental fees were quickly solved by once again renting the space to outside organizations. The tenants have included the United States–New Zealand Council, the Asia Forum–Japan, and the Africa Forum.

The Smithsonian Institution Resident Associates Program regularly includes DACOR Bacon House, together with Octagon House, Woodrow Wilson House, Anderson House, and Meridian House, on tours of Washington's premier historic homes. These tours serve constantly to remind visitors of the people who, from the beginning of the Republic, helped to influence the judicial, diplomatic, congressional, cultural, and social history of our nation.

Together, the variety of programs sponsored by DACOR and the foundation (see pages 142–43) offer a broad learning experience to a wide audience. The satisfaction and enjoyment of that experience are markedly enhanced by the historical ambiance of their venue, DACOR Bacon House, in the midst of one of the city's preeminent collections of American, European, and oriental arts, both fine and decorative. Such an ambiance underscores the interdependent nature of our world and the importance of peaceful cooperation if we are to achieve greater international understanding.

CHAPTER NINE

DACOR BACON HOUSE TODAY

DACOR BACON HOUSE clearly exudes a sense of our nation's early history. During the 1985–86 restoration an effort was made to showcase and illuminate that history. To ensure authenticity, the DACOR team gathered and studied old photographs, inventories, and household records. It also took into account the lore of the house, as recounted by some of Virginia Bacon's family members and friends. Drawing on this reservoir of information, the hundreds of disparate pieces of furniture and decorative objects were assembled into an elegant and workable recreation of a nineteenth-century Federal house. Much of the furniture is of English origin, with a touch of orientalia in most of the rooms. The furnishings have been gathered from countries all over the globe.

One's introduction to the historic house occurs when the oversized leaded-glass front door opens to reveal the small vestibule with its Grecian-style beige-and-white tile floor. Simple but elegant, the vestibule is sparsely furnished with a Victorian umbrella stand, a Chinese red leather bridal chest, an eighteenth-century Dutch prelate's chair, and, in the corner, an elephant's foot. The foot was salvaged from an elephant killed by President Theodore Roosevelt in 1909, one year after leaving the White House, when he led an African safari sponsored by the National Geographic Society.

The garden features a large brick area for entertaining guests. The carriage house and Bacon-era porch are visible in the background. [C. E. Anderson, DACOR Bacon House Foundation Collection]

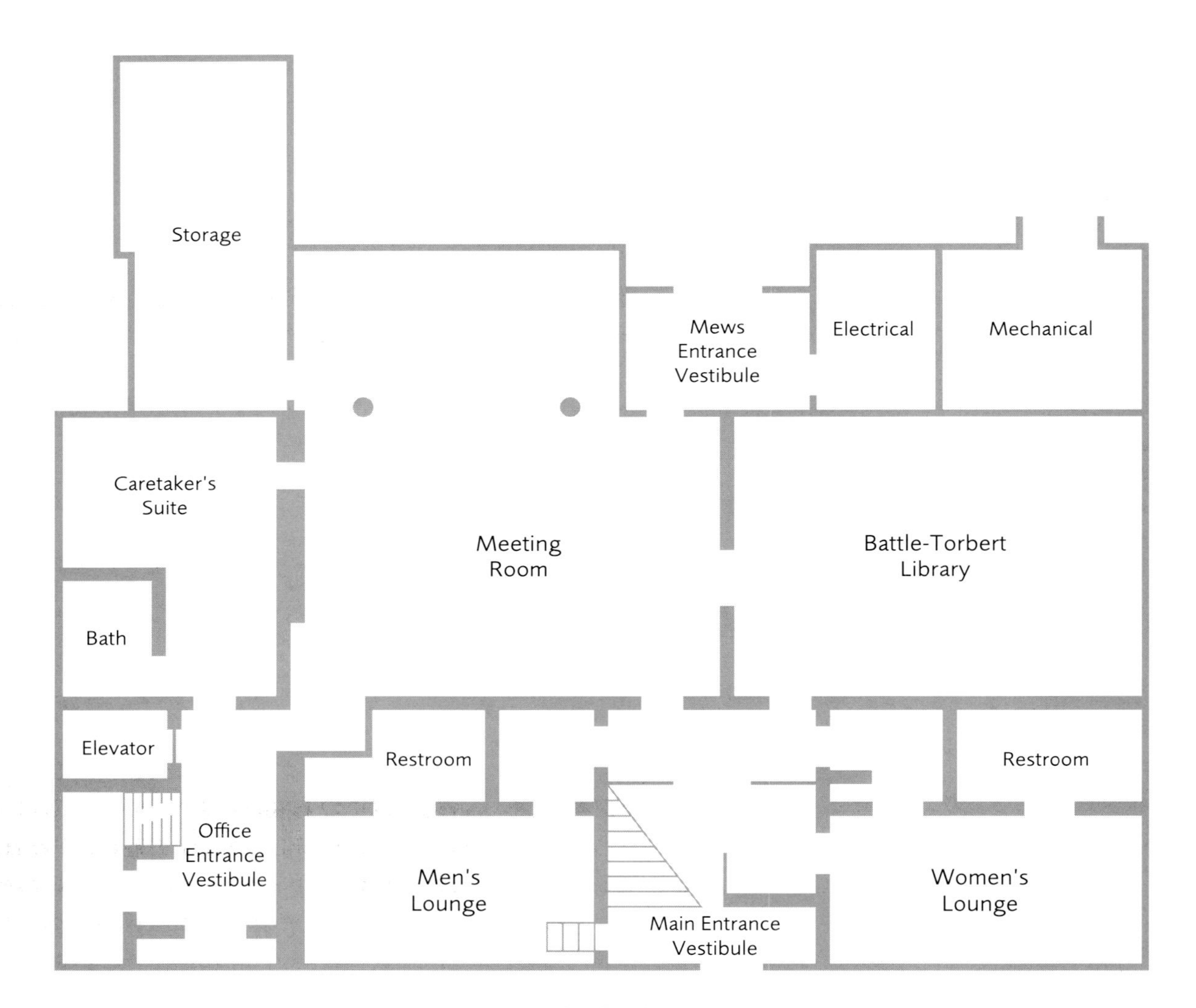
Storage
Mews
Entrance
Vestibule
Electrical
Mechanical
Caretaker's
Suite
Meeting
Room
Battle-Torbert
Library
Bath
Elevator
Restroom
Restroom
Office
Entrance
Vestibule
Men's
Lounge
Main Entrance
Vestibule
Women's
Lounge

FIRST FLOOR

To the right of the entrance foyer is the women's cloakroom-lounge. A hand-knotted Persian Saruk rug delineates a seating area furnished with a variety of nineteenth-century pieces. These include a Regency sofa and tufted-back arm chair, a vanity and bench below a mahogany-and-gilt-framed mirror, and a carved marble-top side table. On the walls are a series of nineteenth-century silhouettes, two circa 1950 Bolivian silver–framed mirrors, and a gilt-bronze wall light. A pair of French Louis XV gilt-bronze candlesticks stand on the vanity. Prominently displayed are the matched portraits of Representative Robert Low Bacon and Virginia Murray Bacon, both in oil and pastel on burlap, painted in the late 1920s by the American artist Robert Reid.

On the opposite side of the foyer is the men's cloakroom-lounge. Grouped around a Fereghan rug are various nineteenth-century furnishings, including a Flemish burl-mahogany, slant-top bureau desk; a walnut library trestle table, above which hangs a large Dutch giltwood-framed mirror; two Philadelphia Chippendale side chairs; and a fine circa 1850 Kuwaiti brass-ornamented, lift-top chest. A series of color and black-and-white engravings, all from the period 1832–60, depict scenes of Washington, D.C.

The DACOR Bacon House Foundation renovation converted much of the first floor to usable entertainment space suitable for a variety of occasions.

Paired at the far end of the room are busts of Robert Bacon Sr., a former secretary of state, and his son. The bust of the father was sculpted in 1918 by James Earle Fraser. The son's is a late 1920s work by Malvina Hoffman. Of special interest is the framed copy of Andrew Ellicott's map entitled *Territory of Columbia,* which was drawn at the request of George Washington, adopted by Congress as the blueprint for the emerging new capital, and published in 1793 in Philadelphia.

Past these antique-filled cloakrooms are DACOR's meeting room and library, also on the ground floor. The meeting room, with a bank of windows overlooking the bricked and landscaped mews, is a large commons room, where members and their guests can relax on comfortable sofas and chairs. Over the oak refectory table, around which Dacorians have gathered for fifty years, hangs a portrait of George Washington painted by Robert Fulton, the noted inventor. It is flanked by a series of nineteenth-century color lithographs depicting scenes of the capital city. On another wall hangs a portrait of Benjamin Franklin, a copy of Pierre Michel Alix's nineteenth-century original, which hangs in the National Portrait Gallery in Washington, D.C. Paired with the Franklin portrait are two circa 1840 oil paintings by George Chinnery depicting Chinese war junks off the China coast. In a small vestibule, beyond the Chelsea brass clock rescued from a World War II U.S. warship, hangs a print of George Washington's hand-written letter, dated December 1787, to Emperor Mohammed III of Morocco. On the wall of the meeting room's alcove is the honor roll of benefactors who for a half century have made special contributions in support of DACOR's educational endeavors.

Amid this art and memorabilia, period furnishings dating mostly from the nineteenth century have been grouped for intimate conversation: two end tables, one an Italian walnut piece with an H stretcher, the other an English piece with William and Mary feet; two sofas; a pair of Chinese Ch'ing yellow mallet-vase table lamps; a pair of heavily carved high-backed English arm chairs; an African drum table; a French leather screen painted with a mythological landscape; and an Italian Renaissance-style bronze torchère floor lamp. Contemporary but prized reminders of organizational roots are photographs of Dacorians past and present, gathered to mark milestones in DACOR's efforts to foster international understanding.

One's sense of history is further heightened on entering the Battle-Torbert library, named for Ambassadors Lucius D. Battle and Horace G. Torbert Jr. There, one is surrounded by two thousand books recounting our nation's diplomatic history, many authored by Dacorians, and by autographed photographs of world leaders laboring to resolve some of the greatest threats to world peace in the twentieth century.

Holding court from his place of honor above the original 1825 fireplace is a photoengraving of Chief Justice John Marshall (see page 119). Below Marshall's portrait, on the mantel, rests a circa 1810 French Empire striking clock in a Grecian temple case. Flanking the fireplace are a series of photographs depicting the area around the White House from 1830 to 1930, as well as photographs of twenty past presidents of DACOR and the DACOR Bacon House Foundation.

A piece that always attracts attention is the circa 1800 ship model of an English man-of-war. A three-masted, 124-gun galleon, the model was made by British prisoners during the Napoleonic wars. In addition to wood the prisoners used animal bone, whales' teeth, iron, ivory, and human hair to make the hundreds of individual pieces needed to create this masterwork. Much admired, the ship rides at anchor atop a circa 1880 continental slant-top writing desk.

Also on display are such diverse articles as the pen used by President

Herbert Hoover in 1930 to sign the Keyes-Elliott bill, an 1841 copy of the Declaration of Independence, a U.S. passport issued in 1873 and signed by Secretary of State Hamilton Fish, and copies of the congressional acts of July 27, 1789, creating the Department of Foreign Affairs, and of September 15, 1789, changing the name to the Department of State. One of the most historic pieces is an Empire desk made in 1823 and used by every secretary of state from John Adams, who served from 1817 to 1825, to Christian Herter, who served from 1959 to 1961. Also of interest are a Victorian magazine rack; two nineteenth-century Pembroke drop-leaf tables; a pair of blue-and-white Chinese Ch'ing dynasty table lamps; and two English, Tudor-style joined pieces, a stool and a bench.

From the front door a wide carpeted staircase sweeps upward between walls glazed magnolia green above a faux-walnut wainscot, past the midlevel, bay-windowed landing festooned with ceremonial flags, to the second-floor receiving area, lined with colorful Chinese ancestral portraits. There one catches the first glimpse of the hierarchy of formal, finely detailed entertainment rooms that are the setting for most of the foundation's educational and cultural programs. From this vantage point one may experience a sense of awe at the grandeur of the principal rooms.

Generously proportioned and high-ceilinged, the rooms are uniformly bathed in a glow from oyster-shell walls heavily accented with glazed architectural moldings and cornices. The reflection from various mirrors serves to enhance the general feeling of spaciousness, as does the sweep of the tall windows crowned with flared pagoda valances and draped with tassel-trimmed, olive-gold silk held in flowing swaths by acanthus leaf tiebacks. Red rugs on coffee-brown hardwood floors delineate seating areas clustered around an exquisite collection of antique furniture and accessories.

The north drawing room, the pivotal unit of the five-room suite, is dominated by a black marble fireplace, above which hangs a magnificent circa 1760 English giltwood mirror. The expertly carved frame, with its rococo and Chinese ornamentation, is reputed to be the work of Thomas Johnson, a talented contemporary of the great Thomas Chippendale. At the center of the room a circa 1840 eight-branch gaslight-and-candle chandelier serves as a point from which one surveys an arresting group of portraits. Two portraits are of Adam and Abigail Babcock, copied in 1900 from the John Singleton Copley originals painted one year before the country declared its independence (see pages 134–35). A 1928 Steinway grand piano, strategically placed so that performing artists can be seen from almost every corner of the area, fills the house with both popular and classical music at frequent concerts.

Gathered around the fireplace is a melange of nineteenth-century English furniture, including a pair of George IV settees and two complementary Georgian open-arm chairs, two upholstered benches, and a set of six Queen Anne chinoiserie and japanned arm and side chairs. An English whatnot, several occasional tables, and a Canterbury music stand offer settings for tablescapes alternately arrayed with flowers, oriental lamps, tea caddies, silver boxes, or dressed for festivities.

The adjacent south drawing room, just slightly smaller, is connected by a wide arch in which nineteenth-century prism-adorned bronze wall sconces hang above period kettle stands displaying antique silver coffee urns. Beyond the arch, the soft walls, stylish window treatments, and red rug reprise those in the larger salon and pull the two rooms together in an uninterrupted continuum. Again, a black marble fireplace with gleaming brass accessories captures the eye. Above it hangs a George I giltwood mirror and on the mantel rests a circa 1790 French striking clock, mounted in a Biedermeier-style, alabaster-columned case. Flanking the clock is a pair of circa 1850 French gilt-bronze, cut-crystal Campagna urns.

The second floor is the primary entertaining area of the house. The open nature of the plan allows for various settings that can accommodate large receptions or small gatherings.

On the opposite wall is a late-eighteenth-century Flemish verdure tapestry depicting a hunting scene. Flanking it are late-nineteenth-century portraits of Peter Crary and Elizabeth Crary, ancestors of Virginia Bacon (see pages 129–31), under which stand two tables—one a George III gaming piece, the other an antique Pembroke drop-leaf—on which are grouped fine Regency lamps, various art objects, and photographs. On either side of the windows at the far end of the room hang portraits of the fourth earl of Dunmore and his wife, Lady Charlotte (see pages 81 and 126–27). Paired below them are an Italian marquetry console and an English block-front sideboard, both of nineteenth-century vintage, on which are arrayed antique oxblood lamps and a melange of photographs of Bacon family members and friends.

More antique furniture is grouped between the fireplace and the tapestry wall, including two sofas, a bishop's crook armchair, a circa 1720 Portuguese black-lacquered side chair, an English barrel-back wing chair, and a fireplace bench. Scattered about on occasional tables, an English whatnot, and a nest of chinoiserie tables are such diverse objects as a Cambodian silver Athenienne perfume burner, a Japanese Imari bowl,

SECOND FLOOR

and a pair of seventeenth-century wine vessels. Also displayed are a Chinese blanc-de-chin Kuan Yin (goddess of mercy) statue, Tibetan musical horns, two Italian miniature oil-on-pearl landscapes, and various silver presentation boxes.

Exquisite eighteenth-century Chinese coromandel screens stand like sentinels guarding the wide arch that joins the north drawing room to the dining room. Within the arch are large track-mounted doors, which can be left partly open, closed, or recessed into the walls to provide openness or intimacy as desired. Comfortably proportioned and seating thirty-six people, the dining room has a warm ambiance created by the Victorian-style candle chandelier, the silver wall sconces, and the indirect lighting hidden behind the marbleized cornice.

The black marble fireplace, a duplicate of the one in the adjoining north salon, first draws one's attention. Over it is a charming portrait of Virginia Bacon at age four (see page 140). Below it, on the mantel, is a circa 1790 English chiming clock, mounted in a brass sphere and topped with a bronze spread-winged eagle. Flanking the clock are a pair of circa 1940 Spanish silver pheasants and a pair of circa 1850 French gilt-bronze and cut-crystal Campagna urns. Around the room are four other large portraits of Virginia Bacon's ancestors, including her father, Henry A. Murray, and her maternal grandfather, Samuel Denison Babcock (see page 138).

The furnishings, all from the nineteenth century, are an eclectic mix: a carved Italian round table extendable to fourteen feet, a baroque Italian sideboard, an English Marlborough-footed serving table, and twenty-two American loop-back side chairs. An ever-changing array of tableware is always on display, some of the more important pieces being an 1884 English silver tea and coffee set, an early-twentieth-century Irish cut-glass punch bowl, and a beautiful pair of late-nineteenth-century Irish crystal candelabra. Chinese coromandel screens to the left and right of the fireplace partially block the adjoining kitchen from view.

The forty-four-foot-long gallery runs the full length of the dining room and the north drawing room. It is connected to both rooms by floor-to-ceiling, double-hung windows resting on chair-rail-height Dutch-door bottoms. Banks of windows wrap around three sides of the gallery, thus providing light, views, and a pleasant transition to the New Orleans–style back porch and garden beyond. A favorite eating place, the gallery has a Victorian wild rose carpet and full-length lace curtains at the windows, which overlook the mews and the carriage house.

President Theodore Roosevelt sent copies of this photoengraving of John Marshall to each justice of the Supreme Court as a Christmas gift in 1901. The 1808 original was by Charles B. J. F. Saint-Mémin. [C. E. Anderson, DACOR Bacon House Foundation Collection]

On the inside wall of the gallery is a large oil-on-canvas landscape in the manner of Fragonard, which is flanked by antique giltwood-framed mirrors. At either end of the gallery hang circa 1784 engravings of Benjamin Franklin—one at the French court, the other at the English court—where he distinguished himself as our country's first diplomat. Adjustable inset ceiling fixtures provide lighting of choice for different occasions, as do Indian brass floor lamps, which add both decoration and a homelike atmosphere.

The garden room at the front of the house is the fifth entertainment area. Virginia Bacon's favorite retreat, it is where she preferred to entertain her closest friends at tea or gather her collaborators to discuss ways to support the artistic and cultural community. The room's special appeal is initially created by the green-glazed and molding-accented walls painted by the British master glazier Malcolm Robson. At the far end of the room is the original fireplace, painted in the same green glaze and fitted with a nineteenth-century English brass-and-iron coal grate. Over the fireplace hangs Constance Curtis's 1905 portrait of Virginia Bacon at the age of sixteen (see page 140), and on the mantel are a pair of antique etched, blown-glass hurricane globes and a malachite-handle Japanese ceremonial samurai sword.

Paired in front of the fireplace are an English Victorian sewing table and a Dutch marquetry book stand. An English secretary (a combination bureau, desk, and bookcase), with a collection of more than 150 leather-bound books, some two hundred years old, is a perennial attraction. So too, on the opposite side of the window, is the circa 1810 Sheraton gaming table, above which hangs a French Louis XVI, giltwood-cased thermometer-barometer by Sormany of Paris.

Clustered on the wall opposite the fireplace is a melange of nineteenth-century engravings and lithographs of American heroes, including George Washington, John Quincy Adams, John Marshall, Andrew Jackson, and Abraham Lincoln. Sharing honors are two framed letters, one dated October 12, 1800, and signed by Lord Murray, the last royal governor of Virginia, the other dated October 29, 1824, and signed by Peter Crary. Also of interest are the silhouettes and engravings of the

Supreme Court personages most closely tied to the history of DACOR Bacon House, namely Chief Justices John Marshall, Melville Weston Fuller, and Edward Douglass White Jr., and Associate Justice Joseph Story. Grouped on the wall opposite the window are five circa 1850 Chinese eglomise genre paintings (reverse painting on glass), a second Japanese ceremonial samurai sword bearing the Tokugawa shogunate crest, a polychrome Kuan Yin figurine, and an intricately carved Chinese altar piece enshrining a carved polychrome Buddha.

Centered among these art treasures, and partly set off by nineteenth-century Chinese coromandel screens, are a camelback settee, two open-arm chairs, a Martha Washington lolling chair, and a late-nineteenth-century Hepplewhite side chair. Complementing these pieces are a Hepplewhite-style coffee table topped with a circa 1890 silver tray, a pair of rosewood and mahogany end tables inlaid with ivory, and a nineteenth-century tilt-top candle stand with an inlaid eagle medallion. A pair of English red-glazed ceramic lamps and a Samson armorial table lamp round out the assemblage.

The third floor is used as office space for various tenants. The offices provide generous space and a convenient location in downtown Washington, D.C.

The third and fourth floors, like the second, are reachable by an elevator or by two staircases—one the original staircase built in 1825, the other a fireproof staircase built into the west wing during the 1985–86 renovation. The 1825 staircase is lined from the second-floor vestibule to the fourth-floor landing with an extraordinary collection of nineteenth-century engravings and lithographs of fourteen presidents of the United States, one secretary of state, and several World War I principals. Displayed at the third-floor landing is an engraving entitled *The British Surrender Their Arms to General Washington after Their Defeat at York Town in Virginia, October 1781*. Nearby is an 1848 engraving entitled *The First Prayer in Congress, September 1773, In Carpenters Hall, Phil.* At the uppermost level hangs a large eighteenth-century oil painting of the angel Gabriel, fashioned in the Angels of Cuzco tradition of the Peruvian city of Cuzco, in which the artistic vogue originated. The painting, which depicts a winged soldier-angel in elaborate period dress brandishing a sword, is believed to have once adorned a church or private chapel in South America.

DACOR offices occupy the fourth floor in conjunction with three guest suites. The Carroll bedroom is currently being used as the executive director's office.

The configuration of the third floor is in all important respects a duplicate of the second floor, with the same high ceilings, tall windows, and full carpeting. The nonprofit organizations currently renting this prime space have provided their own furnishings and decorations, mostly antiques that blend well with the nineteenth-century theme permeating the rest of

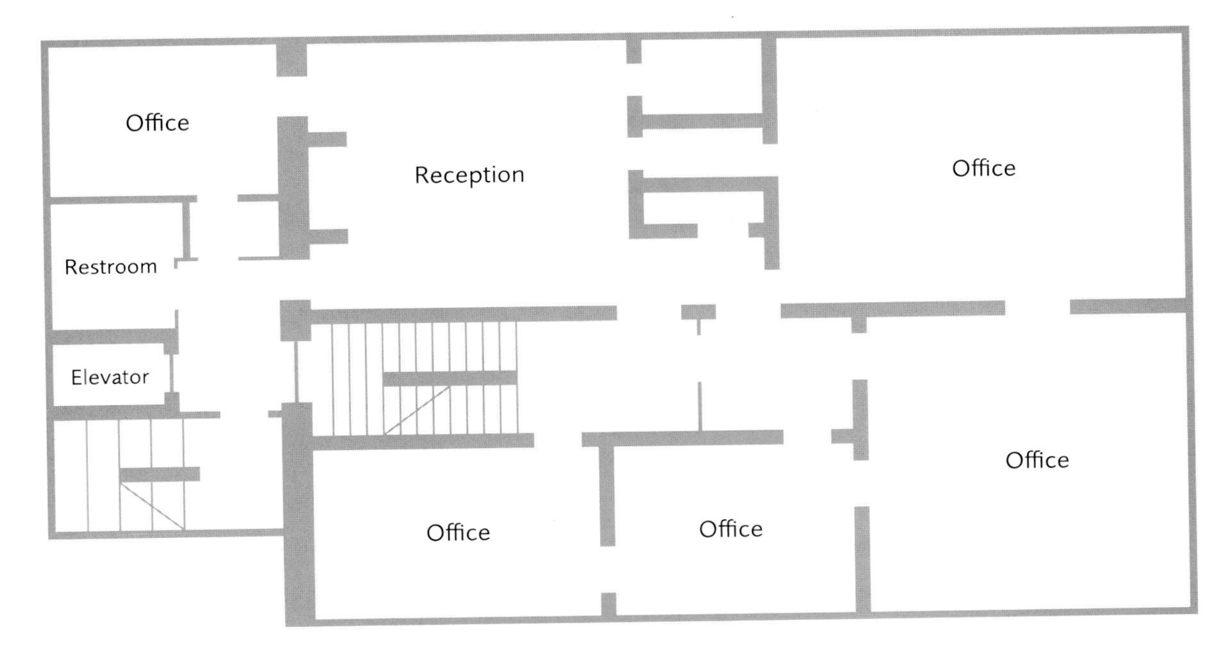

THIRD FLOOR

FOURTH FLOOR

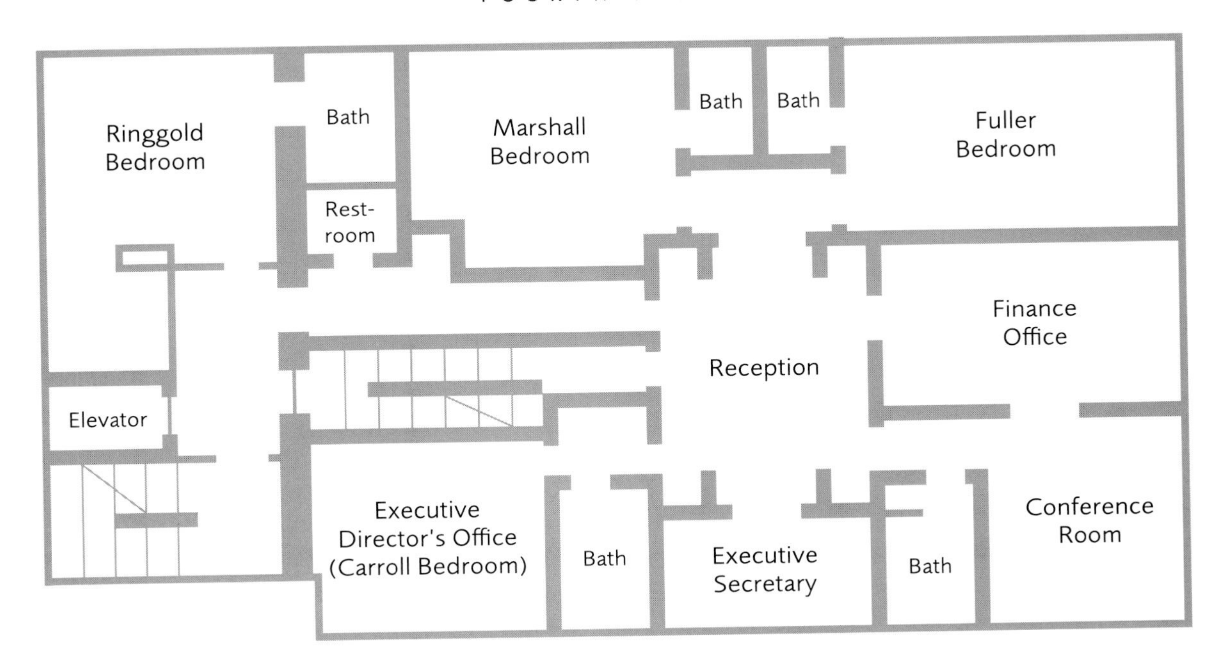

the house. Adding to the charm of these period rooms are furnishings, paintings, and other works of art loaned to the current tenants by the foundation. Among these are a nineteenth-century George V breakfront, a carved Chinese rosewood chest, and a pair of Chinese Chippendale rosewood end tables. Among the art works are two large Chinese paintings on silk from the Ch'ing dynasty, the chromo print *Washington's Grand Entry into New York, Nov. 28, 1783,* and a pair of fine early-twentieth-century watercolors painted in Paris by C. Hoffbauer.

The fourth floor, completely renovated, is divided into five bedrooms, each with a full private bath used by visiting Dacorians. Warm colors, high ceilings, and handsome window treatments imbue each of these rooms with a sense of elegance, just as an eclectic mix of antique and contemporary furnishings conveys a sense of pleasant practicality and comfort. Three of the bedrooms have been named for three previous owners of the mansion, namely the Tench Ringgolds, the Melville Weston Fullers, and the William Thomas Carrolls. The fourth bedroom is named for Chief Justice John Marshall. The fifth bedroom, never named, has from the beginning been a part of the DACOR office suite. If it were to be converted to use as a bedroom, it would no doubt be called the Bacon room. Since 1996 the Carroll bedroom has also been used for office purposes, although it is still called the Carroll room.

Antique and near-antique furniture and accessories adorn each individually decorated bedroom. Among the more noteworthy pieces are an 1892 Currier and Ives print of Washington, D.C., and a trio of late-nineteenth-century color prints depicting the participants, among them Secretary of State John W. Foster, at the United States–Japan Peace Conference negotiating the end of the 1894–95 Sino-Japanese War. Other unusual articles are a trio of Theodore Roosevelt's Rough Riders in a watercolor by Howard C. Christy, an 1840 needlepoint map of France, and a set of six circa 1840 Chinese genre paintings. The 1838 paper-cutout silhouette, *Celebration of American Independence,* by a Miss Eliza S. Jobs of New York, and a map of *Andalvziae* (Andalusia, Spain), believed to have been drawn in 1579, are both one-of-a-kind treasures.

Also featured are a set of four *Washington Series* prints by Charles Magnus depicting prominent landmark buildings in Washington, D.C., in 1864 and an eighteenth-century print of George Washington and his cabinet, comprising Secretary of War Henry Knox, Secretary of the Treasury Alexander Hamilton, Secretary of State Thomas Jefferson, and

Attorney General Edmund Randolph. The single most important piece of furniture is a nineteenth-century Louis XV lady's writing desk with extensive marquetry and ormolu trim. It stands in the vestibule at the elevator entrance to the fourth-floor suite.

The entertainment rooms on the first and second floors and the three bedrooms on the fourth floor are remarkably true to their nineteenth-century roots while evoking a note of freshness and modern-day utility. Their overall appeal lies partly in their conventional elegance and partly in their unexpected eccentricity, creating an ambiance that is both welcoming and comforting. And the beauty of the impeccably arranged rooms is that they are as comfortable for a few people engaged in quiet conversation as they are pleasant for two hundred people mingling at a formal reception.

Not until 1988, two years after occupying the house, did the DACOR Bacon House Foundation turn its attention to restoring the garden. Unfortunately, the garden had suffered from neglect from the time of Virginia Bacon's death in 1980 to the completion of the house renovation in 1986. The trees had survived, as had the wisteria vines and some of the boxwood shrubs, but the rest of the garden was lost. The challenge the foundation faced was to recreate the restful and inviting garden of years past while making it a functional entertainment space suitable for gatherings of several hundred people.

John Shaffer, a professional, award-winning landscape architect, was engaged to oversee the project. He devised a wall on a line with the carriage house to divide the garden into two distinct sections. On one side he created a formal entertainment garden and on the other an out-of-sight service area. For practical reasons, most of the two areas were paved in brick. However, to ensure that the network of tree roots that spread throughout the garden would be properly irrigated, the bricks were laid without mortar on a base of crushed granite. Slate accent strips were used to create borders and divide the common area into attractive geometric patterns. A new larger pergola replaced the original one, by then in a state of collapse.

Much admired are six wrought-iron lattices made for DACOR by Amish craftsmen and installed in 1988. Four of these lattices line the east fringe of the garden and provide a setting for four grayish green stone statues. Representing the four seasons, the statues were purchased at auction in 1988 from an Upperville, Virginia, estate. The other two lattices adorn the west fringe and hold two large stone urns that overflow for much of the year with trailing vines and seasonal flowers.

Placed at strategic points are various decorative accessories. Among them are a nineteenth-century white marble table with spool legs mounted on reclining lions, a Chinese fourteenth-century Martaban (talking) jar, two pairs of ceramic elephant accent tables, and assorted teak and pottery planters. The Bacons' garden furniture is still in use. Periodically refinished (most recently in 1996) and scattered in seating arrangements under the sheltering boughs of the great oak tree, the furniture both enhances and shows off the garden.[1]

The garden in the 1940s was mostly grass and the house was swathed in ivy (above). Today the grass has been removed in favor of soft-laid brick and the ivy has been painstakingly removed from the house (opposite). [DACOR Bacon House Foundation Collection; C. E. Anderson, DACOR Bacon House Foundation Collection]

From the standpoint of both form and function, the garden is a perfect outdoor room for entertaining. In 1988, to extend the magic of daylight into the evening hours, a system of "moonlight" illumination was installed. Hidden in the trees, soft lights reflect off the glossy green magnolia leaves to create a genial air that puts people at ease. From April through October, the garden is the preferred gathering place for Dacorians and their guests before luncheons or during breaks from seminar deliberations and is the setting of choice for weddings and special celebrations.[2]

On viewing the garden for the first time, most visitors are amazed to find so large and verdant a garden in downtown Washington. On a Sunday afternoon, as the noise of a bustling capital seems to be on hold, a countrylike quiet pervades the environs. During the week that peace and tranquillity are sometimes interrupted by the murmur of passing cars and the hum of bureaucratic life. Nevertheless, while sitting surrounded by greenery one can sense the whispers of an adventurous and glamorous past. The garden always has been, and no doubt always will be, one of the most pleasant aspects of life at 1801 F Street. Well conceived, often changed, and generally well attended, the garden has endured more than 170 years through six successive ownerships.

In its restored and recycled form, DACOR Bacon House reflects authenticity in its architectural integrity and art in its craftsmanship. Having dug through the layers of remodeling and modernization dating back to the beginnings of this historic home in 1824–25, the DACOR Bacon House Foundation has restored, to the extent possible, its early-nineteenth-century look and feel. The interior was changed only as necessary to reflect the functional needs of an active, modern-day educational organization, much as the changes made in the previous century and a half reflected the uses, tastes, lifestyles, and fortunes of the earlier owners.

Today the house is experiencing some of the liveliest moments in its long history, although to the casual observer life at the house may appear little changed from its days as a private home. As the pace of activity escalates, DACOR Bacon House remains an elegant setting renowned for intellectual rapport, cultural enlightenment, and grand entertainment.

THE DACOR BACON HOUSE PORTRAITS

Lady Charlotte Stewart Murray's portrait was painted by John Russell in 1765. Lady Charlotte was the wife of the fourth earl of Dunmore, who was the last royal governor-general of the colony of Virginia. [Frick Art Reference Library]

VIRGINIA MURRAY BACON'S ancestors are well represented in portraits in the various entertainment rooms of DACOR Bacon House. The full-length portrait *John Murray, Fourth Earl of Dunmore* (see page 81), depicting her paternal great-great-grandfather resplendent in Stuart tartan kilt, is a copy of an original painted in 1765. It hangs in the south drawing room, as does its companion, *Lady Charlotte Stewart,* a John Russell 1765 portrait of the earl's wife. In the same room hang the circa 1900 portraits *Peter Crary* and *Elizabeth (née Denison) Crary,* both by Otto Merkel and based on Samuel L. Waldo's 1830 originals.

In the north drawing room are the portraits *Richard L. Franklin* and *Evelena (née Crary) Franklin,* painted in 1849 by George Augustus Baker, as well as the portrait *U.S. Representative Robert Low Bacon* (see page 79), painted in 1931 by Jacob Binder. Across the room from each other are the portraits *Adam Babcock* and *Abigail (née Smith) Babcock,* both 1979 copies painted by Adrian Lamb from John Singleton Copley's 1775 originals.

Also in the north drawing room are eleven eighteenth- and nineteenth-century miniatures of various Murray family members. Among them is *Lady Charlotte Stewart Murray.* Others include *Lt. Colonel Alexander Murray and His Wife, Deborah Hunt Murray,* a portrait of of Virginia Bacon's paternal great-grandfather, as well as depictions of several of their

Lady Susan Murray (left), the wife of George Murray, the fifth earl of Dunmore, sat for Sir Thomas Lawrence in the early nineteenth century. [Frick Art Reference Library]

Shown in a miniature of the nineteenth-century British school, the Honorable Alexander Murray (opposite), the second son of Lady Charlotte and John Murray, was Virginia Bacon's paternal great-grandfather. [Frick Art Reference Library]

children: Charlotte, who became the Countess of Derby; Augusta, who married Prince Louis de la Tremoville; and Virginia (see page 82), who died a spinster at the age of sixty-eight. Other miniatures are of Alexander Henry and Alexandrine Amelia, children of the Princess de la Tremoville, and of Lady Borodell, the daughter of an Irish peer and wife of Virginia Bacon's great-uncle, George Denison.

Six portraits hang in the dining room. The largest, *Lady Augusta Murray,* painted in 1775 by George Romney, is of the fourth earl of Dunmore's oldest daughter. Seated on her lap is her young son, Augustus Frederick d'Este (first cousin of Queen Victoria), a child of Lady Augusta's morganatic marriage to Prince Augustus Frederick, the youngest son of

George III. Also exhibited are William Thorne's 1889 portrait *Henry Alexander Murray,* of Virginia Bacon's father; Daniel Huntington's 1894 portrait *Samuel Denison Babcock,* of her maternal grandfather; and William Thorne's 1898 portrait *Maria Babcock,* of one of Samuel Babcock's seven daughters. Sir Thomas Lawrence's early-nineteenth-century portrait *Lady Susan, Wife of George Murray, Fifth Earl of Dunmore,* hangs near the arch leading to the north drawing room. In the adjoining garden room, over the fireplace mantel, Constance Curtiss's 1905 portrait *Virginia Bacon at Age Sixteen* dominates the scene. *Representative Robert Low Bacon* and *Virginia Bacon,* matching pastels painted on burlap in 1925 by Robert Reid, hang in the women's cloakroom.[1]

Behind each of these portraits is an interesting story. For example, the portrait of John Murray, who was the last British governor of the colony of Virginia, is a copy of John Russell's 1765 original owned by the National Portrait Gallery of Scotland. In 1976 the National Gallery of Art in Washington, D.C., borrowed that work to form part of the exhibition called *The Eye of Thomas Jefferson.* Through portraits, paintings, and objects, the exhibition portrayed life as Jefferson witnessed it in the second half of the eighteenth century and first quarter of the nineteenth century. Virginia Bacon was delighted that her paternal great-great-grandfather Murray's portrait was one of the highlights of that exhibition. Seizing the opportunity, she obtained permission from both museums for Winifred Gordon of Baltimore to copy it. The resulting portrait has occupied a prominent position in the south drawing room ever since.[2]

Otto Merkel's circa 1900 portraits of Peter and Elizabeth Crary in the south drawing room and George Augustus Baker's 1849 portraits of Richard and Evelena Franklin in the north drawing room recall the saga of one of New York City's early-nineteenth-century mercantile families. It is a tale that also included Virginia Bacon's maternal ancestors, Benjamin Franklin Babcock and Samuel Denison Babcock.[3]

Shortly after moving from Stonington, Connecticut, to New York City in 1800, Peter Crary and his older brother, Edward, established a dry-goods business, E. and P. Crary, at 107 William Street. Their venture flourished, prompting them and another brother, John, to reincorporate in 1812 as P., E. and J. S. Crary, importers of merchandise from all over the world, especially China and France. Their success enabled the brothers to live in

20692

20691

Peter Crary was painted by Otto Merkel about 1900 after Samuel L. Waldo's 1830 original. Crary was a New York merchant in the early nineteenth century. [Frick Art Reference Library]

Elizabeth Denison Crary was the wife of Peter Crary and one of Virginia Bacon's great-aunts. Her portrait by Otto Merkel about 1900 is after Samuel L. Waldo's 1830 original. [Frick Art Reference Library]

Richard L. Franklin married Evelena Crary, daughter of Peter and Elizabeth Crary. George Augustus Baker painted him in 1849. [Frick Art Reference Library]

Evelena Crary Franklin, daughter of Peter and Elizabeth Crary, was the wife of Richard L. Franklin. Her portrait by George Augustus Baker also dates from 1849. [Frick Art Reference Library]

high style and maintain large houses. Grateful for their good fortune and spurred by a deep sense of patriotism, they loaned the U.S. government $10,000 to help finance the War of 1812.

In 1816 the brothers reorganized as Crarys and Babcock with a new partner, Benjamin Franklin Babcock of Rhode Island. In 1818 the firm dissolved, Edward retired well off, Babcock went his separate way, and the two remaining brothers continued as P. and J. S. Crary, operating at 177 Pearl Street, where years earlier John Jacob Astor had maintained an establishment. In 1824 Peter and John took as their partner Oliver Ellsworth Cobb, and together the three operated as P. and J. S. Crary and Company until the crash of 1837 wiped them out. Peter Crary died at Belleville, New Jersey, in 1842, a broken man.

Peter and Elizabeth Crary's daughter, Evelena, married Richard Lawrence Franklin, a hardware merchant of note, first in New York City and later in Flushing, Long Island. Another Crary daughter married James L. Morris, and a Crary son, Edward C., married a daughter of Robert Fulton, who invented the steamboat.[4]

One of the Franklins' daughters, Elizabeth Crary Franklin, married Benjamin Franklin Babcock's son, Samuel Denison Babcock. Their daughter, Fannie Morris Babcock, was Virginia Bacon's mother. Samuel's portrait in the dining room, by Huntington, was until 1994 a source of some confusion. The Frick Art Reference Library in New York City, which tracks the whereabouts and ownership of thousands of artworks in the United States, corresponded with Virginia Bacon and after her death with her curator, Lawrence Kolp, noting that the library's records described the Samuel Babcock portrait in her possession as a gentleman seated holding a pair of eyeglasses. The painting, the library insisted, was the work of William Thorne and was dated 1894. William Thorne, it should be noted, did paint the portrait of Virginia Bacon's Aunt Maria, another of Samuel Babcock's daughters, which also hangs in the dining room.

Virginia Bacon and later Lawrence Kolp gave repeated assurances that the gentleman in the portrait at 1801 F Street was seated holding a book. Moreover, the painting was signed by Daniel Huntington, although the date, 1894, was the same. As late as 1993 the DACOR Bacon House Foundation gave the Frick Library similar assurances and provided photographs to prove the point.

By coincidence, in 1993 Mary M. Thacher, librarian at the Stonington Historical Society of Stonington, Connecticut, was engaged in research to identify the subject of one of the society's fine portraits, that of a gentleman seated holding a pair of glasses. The work was signed William Thorne and dated 1894. Mary Thacher believed the portrait might be of Samuel Babcock. Her research eventually led her to the Frick Art Reference Library and then to DACOR Bacon House. When a photograph of the society's portrait was compared with the one hanging at DACOR Bacon House, the mystery was solved for both the Stonington Historical Society and the Frick Library.

Both portraits, it turns out, had once been in the possession of Virginia Bacon's mother, Fannie Babcock Murray. No one can explain why two portraits of the same subject were painted by different artists within a few months of each other, but perhaps one was commissioned for the family and the other for corporate use. On Fannie Murray's death in 1940, the Huntington portrait passed to her daughter, Virginia Bacon, and the Thorne portrait to her son, Henry A. Murray Jr. of Cambridge, Massachusetts. In 1964 Henry Murray donated the Thorne portrait to the Stonington Historical Society. With changes of personnel over the next thirty years, the identity of the gentleman in the portrait was lost. Today, rediscovered, William Thorne's portrait of Samuel Babcock hangs in the Stonington Free Library—fittingly so, for it was he and his friend, Erskine M. Phelps of Chicago, who donated $8,000 each to build the library in 1900.[5]

The portraits by John Singleton Copley of Adam Babcock and Abigail Babcock were commissioned by the sitters in 1775 and initially displayed in their Boston home. On Adam's death in 1817, the portraits passed to one of their children, and in the next generation to their grandson, the Reverend Edwin A. Blake. In turn, a Miss A. G. Chapman acquired the portraits and eventually sold them to Arthur Meeker of Chicago. In 1926 the portraits were sold on Meeker's behalf by M. Knoedler and Company of New York City. The buyer was Virginia Bacon's mother, Fannie Babcock Murray, who during her lifetime displayed both portraits in her New York home at 955 Park Avenue.

No doubt the sheer joy of possessing original portraits of two of her maternal ancestors was Fannie Murray's motivation for purchasing these paintings. However, she was also a wise connoisseur who was fully aware that each painting was a prized work of American art. The bill of sale documents her understanding that the noted art historian Frank W. Bayley, in his book *The Life and Works of John Singleton Copley* (1915), had judged

Samuel Denison Babcock, Virginia Bacon's maternal grandfather, was painted by Daniel Huntington in 1894. [Frick Art Reference Library]

Maria Babcock, daughter of Samuel Denison Babcock and Virginia Bacon's aunt, was painted by William Thorne in 1898. [Frick Art Reference Library]

the portraits to be "late and very fine examples of Copley's American period." Moreover, she had read Henry van Horn's article "The American Portraits from the Collection of Arthur Meeker, Esq.," which had appeared in the February 21, 1921, issue of *Town and County* magazine. In that article van Horn judged the portrait of Abigail Babcock to be "the finest of Copley's American period," painted shortly before Copley, a staunch Royalist, left America in 1775 for England, where he spent the rest of his life.

In 1979, in a most generous and patriotic gesture, Virginia Bacon and Henry Murray donated the Copley originals to the National Gallery of Art, which, as an expression of appreciation, had copies painted for them by the portraitist Adrian Lamb.[6] Abigail's portrait, first Copley's original and later Lamb's copy, has hung at Bacon House for more than half a century. Adam's portrait, first Copley's original and later Lamb's copy, was displayed at Henry Murray's Cambridge home from 1940 until his death in 1988, when it was inherited by his daughter, Josephine L. Murray. She in turn donated it in 1991 to the DACOR Bacon House Foundation.[7] After a separation of several decades, Adam and Abigail have been doubly reunited—by bringing together John Singleton Copley's 1775

Adam Babcock was the son of Joshua Babcock and Hannah Stanton Babcock. His portrait was painted by Adrian Lamb in 1979 after John Singleton Copley's 1775 original. [Frick Art Reference Library]

originals at the National Gallery of Art and Adrian Lamb's 1979 copies at DACOR Bacon House.

Behind the 1775 George Romney painting *Lady Augusta Murray and Her Son, Sir Augustus Frederick d'Este,* which hangs in the dining room, lies a love story. In his book *Wicked Uncles in Love,* Morris Marples recounts the tale in a chapter entitled "Gussy and Goosy," summarized here.

After Prince Augustus Frederick completed his classical education in England, his father, George III, sent him to Germany at the age of thirteen to study at the University of Göttingen. Following that experience he pursued the broader education found in the customary grand tour. By 1792, at the age of nineteen, he had grown into a tall, handsome, self-assured

Abigail Smith Babcock was the wife of Adam Babcock. Her portrait was painted by Adrian Lamb in 1979 after John Singleton Copley's 1775 original. [Frick Art Reference Library]

young man. While sightseeing at a church in Italy one day he encountered a lady and her two daughters. Noting that the elder daughter's shoe was untied, he knelt to fasten it. Identities were exchanged. The women turned out to be Lady Charlotte, the wife of John Murray, the fourth earl of Dunmore, her eldest daughter, Augusta, and the youngest, Virginia. The prince's request for permission to call on the trio at their hotel was granted, and thus were sown the seeds of romance with Augusta.

Through a series of meetings and a constant flow of letters, the courtship flourished to the point where the prince, declaring that "where Goosy is not, is no pleasure for Augustus," proposed marriage. In doing so he made it clear that because of the restrictions of the Royal Marriage

Act, the king would never consent to his marriage outside the royal blood. In accepting his proposal, Augusta in turn made it clear that she would not accept an irregular union. Both desperate and inspired, Augustus remembered that some years earlier his older brother, the Prince of Wales, had drawn up his own marriage document and, without Crown consent, married the woman he loved. Following this precedent, Augustus prepared his own marriage vows and persuaded a visiting English parson to marry them. For a time they were able to keep the union secret, but when Augusta began to exhibit obvious symptoms of pregnancy, they made known their morganatic marriage.

Prince Augustus's governor, who had accompanied him throughout his travels, urgently reported this development to the king, who ordered his son to return to London. Finding that their return evoked little comment or interference from the royal family, the couple quietly posted banns of marriage for "Mr. Augustus Frederick and Miss Augusta Murray" at St. George's, Hanover Square. No one seemed to notice; if they did, they said nothing. Three weeks later they were wed a second time, because, said Augusta, "she had married Mr. Frederick in Italy when he was under age [she was twenty-nine and he was nineteen]" and so decided to be remarried. Their first baby, a boy (the child in the portrait), was born two weeks later and named Augustus Frederick after his father.

Informed of this latest act of disobedience, the king ordered his son to return to Italy, ostensibly for medical reasons. No sooner had Augustus departed than the king ordered legal proceedings in the Court of Arches, which in due course declared both marriages null and void. Hardly settled in Italy, Augustus was next ordered to proceed to Berlin, no doubt to avoid the war with France. Augusta, who had been ordered to remain in London, traveled on a forged passport and joined her husband in the German capital, where they lived together for the next six years.

In 1800 Augustus, now twenty-seven, was openly frustrated about his father's refusal to grant him a dukedom, to which all royal princes were entitled. Equally important, he wanted the allowance that went with it. This frustration was the catalyst that prompted him to send Lady Augusta and his young son back to London, naively hoping that the king would imagine he and they had parted company. Realizing that the ruse had not worked, Augustus himself returned to England and resumed living with his wife and child. In a surprise move, a few months after the birth in 1801 of their second child, Emma, he sent Augusta a letter announcing his intention to leave her.

Lady Augusta Murray and her son, Augustus Frederick d'Este, were painted by George Romney. [C. E. Anderson, DACOR Bacon House Foundation Collection]

Augusta was given custody of the two children and an annual allowance of £4,000 and by royal license was thereafter called the Countess d'Ameland. Until her death in 1830, she devoted herself to raising the two children and to the hopeless cause of seeking royal acceptance. Prince Augustus was named the duke of Sussex, earl of Inverness, and baron of Arklow and was granted an annual parliamentary allowance of £12,000.

In 1809, offended to learn that the countess had enrolled their son at Harrow under the assumed name of Douglas, the prince sought and was granted legal custody of the two children. Although he paid little attention to them, he did resolve the question of a family name for the children by declaring that henceforth they would be known by the surname d'Este. Lady Augusta would be called Mademoiselle d'Este. She and the prince, it seems, had a common Italian ancestor of that name from whom the children were thus doubly descended.

On leaving school at age eighteen, young Augustus d'Este was commissioned in the Seventh Royal Fusiliers, which fought in the 1815 Battle of New Orleans. His military career was generally stormy, made so by his habit of flaunting his royal pretensions, but he eventually rose to the rank of lieutenant colonel after his father appointed him his equerry. After his mother's death, Augustus d'Este continued to stir fresh assertions of his own importance and royal prerogatives, without success. The final blow came on his father's death, when his claim to the dukedom of Sussex was formally rejected. In 1848, having never married, he died a helpless cripple at the age of fifty-four, a victim of disseminated sclerosis.

Emma, always less concerned than her brother about royal aspirations, married Sir Thomas Wilde, who became Lord Truro and lord chancellor of England. Although she was never recognized as a royal princess, as the wife of a major public figure Emma was a popular and accepted member of English society.

Two years after the death of the Lady Augusta, Augustus married Lady Cecelia Buggin, the widow of Sir George Buggin and daughter of the second earl of Arron. Like his marriage to Lady Augusta, the duke's second marriage was also a morganatic affair, because he had failed (purposely it is thought) to regularize the union as required by the Royal Marriage Act. In these circumstances Lady Cecelia was debarred from styling herself duchess of Sussex. In 1837, however, Queen Victoria, grateful that Augustus (her favorite uncle) had graciously yielded royal precedence to her consort, Prince Albert, dubbed Lady Cecelia duchess of Inverness. The duke and his duchess enjoyed eleven happy years until his death in 1843 at age 71 of erysipelas.[8]

The 1775 George Romney portrait of Lady Augusta and her son, Augustus, passed from her to her daughter, Emma, and then to succeeding heirs until it was bought at auction in London after World War I by Charles W. Schwab, an American industrialist. Three years after Schwab's death in 1939, the painting was put up for auction in New York. This time Virginia Bacon bought it, and the two-hundred-year-old painting came to 1801 F Street, where it has occupied a prominent place in the dining room ever since.[9]

In the library is the portrait *John Marshall,* a 1901 photoengraving of the 1808 original drawn and tinted by Charles B. J. F. Saint-Mémin (see page 119). Saint-Mémin's original hangs in the Duke University Law Library. As in the original, Marshall's left profile, measuring fifteen inches by twenty-four inches, is engraved on pink paper, set off by a black oval mat, and encased in a knotted-maple frame.

Curious about the origin of the engraving, the foundation consulted the National Portrait Gallery in Washington, D.C. After examining it the gallery's experts declared that the portrait was one of the nine copies made in 1901 for President Theodore Roosevelt, who gave them as Christmas presents to the nine sitting justices of the Supreme Court. One recipient was Chief Justice Melville Weston Fuller, then living at 1801 F Street. Another was Associate Justice Edward D. White Jr., whose maternal grandfather, Tench Ringgold, built the house in 1825 and whose mother, Catherine Ringgold, had lived there.

Paul F. DuVivier, the Dacorian who donated the Marshall portrait to the DACOR Bacon House Foundation, related how his father had purchased it in 1906 at auction in Hartford, Connecticut, and displayed it in his law office for more than fifty years. This copy may be the one given to Associate Justice Horace Gray of Massachusetts, who died in 1902 and is the only justice whose tenure on the court ended between 1901 and the

Henry Alexander Murray was Virginia Bacon's father. His portrait by William Thorne was painted in 1889. [Frick Art Reference Library]

1906 auction. Moreover, he was the only justice at that time who called New England home. On presenting Marshall's portrait to the foundation, Paul DuVivier noted: "Marshall belongs at DACOR Bacon House, where he lived and worked in the early 1830s."

A mystery surrounds the portrait entitled *George Washington,* which hangs in the meeting room, a 1997 gift of Therese Symans of Grand Rapids, Michigan (see page 32). She and her husband, Edward A. Symans, had obtained it during his service at the U.S. Embassy in Warsaw in the 1960s. The portrait was said to be of George Washington and to have been painted in Paris in 1804 "from memory" by Robert Fulton, inventor of the steamboat. Handsomely framed, the oil-on-canvas painting is so signed and dated.

While having some doubts about both the identity of the subject and the authenticity of the artist, the Symanses found the portrait quite attractive and bought it. They were aware that Washington had died five years before the portrait's date and seventeen years after Fulton had left the United States to live in Europe. Nevertheless, they also knew that some artists occasionally paint from memory, that Fulton was indeed a resident of Paris in 1804, and that the distinguished gentleman wearing a white shirt, white cravat, white waistcoat, and black coat was realistic enough to be accepted as a vigorous Washington at about the time he became the country's first president.

Some viewers immediately identify the subject as Washington. Others look, ponder, then ask the identity of the gentleman in the portrait. And those who question the identity of the subject also speculate as to whether it is really a work by Fulton. The National Gallery of Art shares some of these doubts but believes that the portrait may be by Fulton. That the gallery's catalogue of fifty known Fulton works includes portraits painted both before and after 1804 but does not list the Washington portrait multiplies the uncertainty. Lettered in pencil on the back of the stretcher is the notation "Renck 1754–1809." Its significance remains a mystery.

Despite the uncertainty surrounding it, the portrait was displayed in the

Symanses' home for thirty-five years. The foundation will take equal pleasure in displaying it at DACOR Bacon House in future decades.

Also displayed at DACOR Bacon House are photographs of two portraits of Virginia Bacon's paternal great-great-great-great-grandparents: Joshua Babcock (1707–78) and his first wife, Hannah Stanton Babcock (1714–78). Painted by Joseph Blackburn, the portraits still exist but hang elsewhere. About them, however, turns an interesting family tale.[10]

Of Joshua and Hannah's several children, their son Adam was a Congregational minister in Brookline, Massachusetts. In this capacity, in the mid-1800s, Adam became interested in the Granary Burying Ground, where he personally supervised the building of a series of brick tombs. For his own use he kept tomb number 36, in which, over time, fourteen members of the Babcock family were buried, including his father, Joshua Babcock, and Joshua's second wife, Martha Hubbard Babcock.

About 1910 Elizabeth Mathews-Richardson, a Babcock descendant, on one of her frequent visits to the family tomb found that the brick front on which "Babcock 36" was cut had fallen out and lay on the ground. At home she mentioned the matter to her mother and indicated that she would arrange to have needed repairs made. She was quite surprised to hear her mother remark that she saw "no special use in doing so since the old tomb for more than a dozen years had been untenanted." Years earlier, her mother explained, when it was feared that a street improvement project might obliterate the tomb, Elizabeth's Uncle George had backed a wagon up to the cemetery wall in the dead of night and transferred all fourteen coffins to a

new resting place in Brookline's Forest Hills Cemetery. The transfer had been made without obtaining permits or notifying the cemetery officials. Because the whole matter might be called body snatching and involve imprisonment and fines, her mother thought it unwise to talk about it.

Elizabeth Mathews-Richardson was upset to learn about this family secret and irritated that she had been allowed to make numerous cemetery pilgrimages to pay her respects to ancestors no longer buried there. Determined that the lost shall be found, she made inquiries at the Forest Hills Cemetery only to be told that no Babcocks were buried there. Inquiries at the Mount Auburn Cemetery brought similar results. Remembering that Uncle George had been involved with the Walnut Hills Cemetery, she next inquired there. "Yes," said the superintendent, "here is Adam, and here is Martha" and twelve others.

Apart from discovering the whereabouts of the missing relatives, a second gratifying result stemmed from this episode. Through the retelling of this experience, Ernest William Bowditch, a member of the extended Babcock family, learned of the existence of two family portraits. Painted about 1760 by Joseph Blackburn, the portraits were of Joshua Babcock and his wife, Hannah, and both were in the possession of Elizabeth Mathews-Richardson's father, the Reverend Mathews. After negotiations Mathews agreed to lend Hannah's portrait to Bowditch so that he might have a copy painted by Ernest Ipsen. No amount of coaxing, however, would convince him to release Joshua's portrait.

Virginia Murray, the future Mrs. Robert Bacon, was painted at age four by William Thorne and at age sixteen by Constance Curtiss. [C. E. Anderson, DACOR Bacon House Foundation Collection]

Years later, after her father's death, Elizabeth Mathews-Richardson offered to sell the portraits. At that point Bowditch, anxious to keep them in the family, bought the portrait of Joshua. After enjoying it for many years in his Milton, Massachusetts, home he donated it to Boston's Museum of Fine Arts. The portrait of Hannah Babcock was purchased by Fannie Babcock Murray of New York City, Virginia Bacon's mother. In 1940 it passed to her son Henry A. Murray Jr. and in 1988 to Henry's widow, Nina, of Cambridge, Massachusetts. On Nina Murray's death, Hannah's portrait, too, will go to the Museum of Fine Arts, to be reunited after a separation of many decades with that of Joshua.

DACOR AND THE DACOR BACON HOUSE FOUNDATION

The historic DACOR Bacon House, convenient to U.S. government centers, cultural landmarks, and international institutions in the nation's capital, houses the headquarters of Diplomatic and Consular Officers, Retired (DACOR) and the DACOR Bacon House Foundation.

Established as a nonprofit educational and cultural institution, the DACOR Bacon House Foundation is a center of excellence in the field of international thought and discourse. It strives to enhance international understanding by regularly bringing together groups of prominent and knowledgeable persons to study, discuss, and reach conclusions about important national and foreign policy issues. Led by diplomats, scholars, and representatives of international organizations, participants seek to develop a consensus of ideas and opinions for a constituency of national leaders engaged in giving shape and substance to U.S. public policy.

Each year the foundation sponsors a conference that explores a timely foreign affairs topic and then publishes and disseminates the full proceedings to Congress, other government legislative offices, universities, and foreign affairs institutions. Through its monthly speaker series and randomly convened colloquia, the foundation provides a forum for the discussion of topics bearing directly on current foreign affairs issues.

A monthly series of Sunday afternoon concerts and musicales explores

the rich heritage of music as an expression of the world's cultural diversity, as revealed both in the quality of the gifted artists featured and in the variety of the music performed.

The foundation offers quarterly seminars for graduate students in international studies at the various Washington-area universities. At these seminars the students meet with foreign affairs professionals and retired American diplomats, who discuss their overseas experiences and share their expertise on subjects within the students' courses of study. Through its educational outreach the foundation also provides fellowships to deserving students. Granted on the basis of academic merit and financial need, these fellowships encourage studies in international relations at both undergraduate and graduate levels.

* * * * *

Diplomatic and Consular Officers, Retired (DACOR), with the support of its more than 2,300 members, is the umbrella organization for the DACOR Bacon House Foundation. Under its own auspices, DACOR sponsors a monthly luncheon series at which members and guests explore a mix of stimulating topics. Speakers might include an author discussing his or her new book, an astronaut describing the future horizons of space flight, a newspaper correspondent relating the problems of covering events in a war-torn region, or a recently returned American ambassador discussing the state of bilateral relations between the United States and his country of assignment.

The organization sponsors the DACOR Memorial Section of Rock Creek Cemetery, where it organizes an annual Memorial Day service. For retired diplomats and their families, this hallowed ground is the equivalent of Arlington National Cemetery for military personnel.

The DACOR research library contains a special collection of two thousand books on the history and practice of diplomacy. Some two hundred of these books were written by Dacorians, many of whom rank among the most influential American diplomats of the twentieth century. Available to Dacorians and scholars, these books recount personal efforts to further world peace as well as the vagaries of living overseas. Beginning in 1995, DACOR has joined with the Association for Diplomatic Studies and Training (ADST) in sponsoring the publication of such books in the ADST-DACOR Diplomats and Diplomacy Series.

NOTES

PROLOGUE. A LANDMARK KEEPSAKE

1. DACOR Bacon House Foundation, *History of the House* [summary] (Washington, D.C.: DACOR Bacon House Foundation, May 1986), 1–4.
2. "Bacon House: Symbol of Grand Elegance," *Washington Times,* April 1, 1994, sec. C, p. 14.
3. Patricia Beard, "Follies," *Town and Country,* April 1993, 109.
4. James M. Goode, *Capital Losses: A Cultural History of Washington's Destroyed Buildings* (Washington, D.C.: Smithsonian Institution Press, 1979), 6–7; Wilhelmus B. Bryan, *A History of the National Capital from Its Foundation through the Period of the Adoption of the Organic Act* (New York: Macmillan, 1914–16), 1:36–43.
5. National Trust for Historic Preservation, easement records, July 1977.
6. Hope Ridings Miller, *Great Houses of Washington, D.C.* (New York: Clarkson N. Potter, 1969), 159.

CHAPTER ONE. THE CAPITAL TAKES FORM, 1721–1814

1. Bryan, *History of the National Capital,* 1:36–43; *Academic American Encyclopedia* (Danbury, Conn.: Grolier, 1992), 6:201.
2. Bryan, *History of the National Capital,* 1:39.
3. Suzanne Hilton, *A Capital Capital City, 1790–1814* (New York: Atheneum Macmillan, 1992), 3–4.
4. Ibid., 5.
5. "The Federal Home Loan Bank Building: Its Effect on the Winder Building and Related Properties" (Washington, D.C.: Advisory Council on Historic Preservation, March 1974), 5.
6. Goode, *Capital Losses*, 6–7; Bryan, *History of the National Capital*, 1:124–35; Constance

McLaughlin Green, *A History of the Capital, 1800–1878 and 1879–1950* (Princeton: Princeton University Press, 1962), 1:1–4.

7. Goode, *Capital Losses*, 6–7, 32–33; *National Cyclopaedia of American Biography* (New York: James T. White, 1892–98), 6:227.

8. DACOR Bacon House Foundation, *History of the House*, 1–4.

9. Bryan, *History of the National Capital*, 1:590–91.

10. Ibid., 1:355–57, 2:1–5, 276–77.

CHAPTER TWO. PROPERTY OF A PRESIDENT'S SECRETARY, 1815–1824

1. Ray A. Brighton, *The Checkered Career of Tobias Lear* (Portsmouth, N.H.: Portsmouth Marine Society, 1985), 16–21.

2. Ibid., 33.

3. Ibid., 32–33.

4. Ibid., 163.

5. Ibid., 124.

6. Ibid., 139.

7. Ibid., 182–93.

8. Ibid., 296.

9. Ibid., 300–301.

10. Ibid., 287, 296–303.

11. Ibid., 305–7.

12. Ibid., 307–8.

13. Ibid., 308–10.

14. Ibid., 312–26.

15. Tobias Lear, *Observations on the River Potomack, the Country Adjacent, and the City of Washington* (New York: Samuel Loudon and Son, 1793), 25–26.

16. Brighton, *Checkered Career*, 324.

17. Ibid., 329.

CHAPTER THREE. MARSHALL AND THE JUSTICES MOVE IN, 1824–1835

1. Elizabeth S. Duvall, *Three Centuries of American Life* (Chestertown, Md.: Kent County Historical Society, 1988), 31–41.

2. Ibid., 49; Bryan, *History of the National Capital*, 1:527.

3. Bryan, *History of the National Capital*, 1:636; Duvall, *Three Centuries*, 49.

4. *Dictionary of American Biography* (New York: Scribner's Sons, 1957–64), 6:107–8.

5. Goode, *Capital Losses*, 20–21.

6. J. L. Sibley Jennings, "Bacon House," [report] J. L. Sibley Jennings, AIA, and Associates, Architects (DACOR Bacon House Foundation, February 1983), 1–4; DACOR Bacon House Foundation, *History of the House*, 1–4.

7. Talbot Hamlin, *Benjamin Henry Latrobe* (New York: Oxford University Press, 1955), 150–52, 196–201.

8. *The Congressional Directory* (Washington, D.C.: U.S. Government Printing Office, 1809, 1831, 1832, and 1833).

9. Albert J. Beveridge, *The Life of John Marshall* (Boston: Houghton Mifflin, 1916–19), 4:86–87.

10. Ibid., 87.
11. Ibid., 88.
12. Clare Cushman, ed., *The Supreme Court Justices: Illustrated Biographies, 1789–1993* (Washington, D.C.: Congressional Quarterly, 1993), 61–65.
13. Ibid., 86–90.
14. *National Cyclopaedia of American Biography,* 10:76. To succeed White as chief justice, President Warren G. Harding appointed former president William Howard Taft, who thus became the only former president ever to later hold the country's highest judicial office.
15. Charles Francis Adams, ed., *Memoirs of John Quincy Adams: Comprising Portions of His Diary from 1795 to 1848* (Philadelphia: J. B. Lippincott, 1874–77), 8:317–19.
16. Ibid., 317.
17. Duvall, *Three Centuries,* 27–41.
18. *Debrett's Peerage and Baronetage* (London: Debrett's Peerage, 1985), 64–67, 389–91.
19. Duvall, *Three Centuries,* 31, 41, 43, 53.
20. Ibid., 37, 39, 40–42.
21. Ibid., 42–46.
22. Ibid., 53.
23. DACOR Bacon House Foundation, *History of the House,* 1–4.

CHAPTER FOUR. RAISING THE ROOF, 1835–1895

1. John Thomas Scharf, *History of Maryland* (Hatboro, Pa.: Tradition Press, 1967), 2:270, 535, 546, 3:148–49, 162; Frank F. White Jr., *Governors of Maryland, 1777–1970* (Annapolis: Maryland Hall of Records Commission, 1970), 78–80; Heinrich E. Buchholz, *Governors of Maryland from the Revolution to the Year 1908* (Baltimore: William and Wilkins, 1908), 91–94; *National Cyclopaedia of American Biography,* 9:300.
2. *Dictionary of American Biography,* 2:522–24, 526–28; *Biographical Cyclopaedia of Representative Men of Maryland and District of Columbia* (Baltimore: National Biographical Publishing Company, 1879), 76–78; Daniel Joseph Boorstin, *The Americans,* vol. 1, *The Colonial Experience* (New York: Random House, 1958–73), 111–16.
3. *Dictionary of American Biography,* 2:522–24, 526–28.
4. Hampton L. Carson, *The Supreme Court of the United States: Its History. Its Centennial Celebration—February 4, 1890* (Philadelphia: A. R. Keller, 1892), 575–76.
5. Historic plaque placed by National Society of Colonial Dames of America, 2715 Q Street, N.W., Washington, D.C.
6. Carson, *Supreme Court of the United States,* 575–76.
7. Alexander L. Stevas, retired clerk of the U.S. Supreme Court, interview by author, May 12, 1994; Public Law 88–279, 88th Congress, H.R. 7235, March 10, 1964.
8. Frederick Haupt III, "Virginia Bacon, Not Ham," *Virginia Country,* February 1987, 90.
9. Alexander L. Stevas, interview by author, October 28, 1996.
10. Haupt, "Virginia Bacon, Not Ham," 90–91; *Appleton's Encyclopaedia of American Biography* (New York: D. Appleton, 1888–1901), 1:539.
11. *Dictionary of American Biography* 2:528–29.
12. Bryan, *History of the National Capital,* 1:496–503.
13. Jennings, "Bacon House," 1–4.

14. Ibid., 1.

15. Mrs. Robert Low Bacon, personal papers, Georgetown University Library. Georgetown University Library owns the most complete set of Virginia Bacon's papers. Copies of selected and uncatalogued papers were retained but not catalogued by the DACOR Bacon House Foundation.

16. Bryson B. Rash, *Footnote Washington: Tracking the Engaging, Humorous and Surprising Bypaths of Capital History* (McLean, Va.: EPM Publications, 1983), 111.

CHAPTER FIVE. ANOTHER CHIEF JUSTICE HOLDS COURT, 1896–1910

1. Willard L. King, *Melville Weston Fuller: Chief Justice of the United States, 1888–1910* (New York: Macmillan, 1950), 152.

2. Ibid., 1–7.

3. Ibid., 10.

4. Ibid., 10–14.

5. Ibid., 28–29.

6. Cushman, *Supreme Court Justices*, 246–50.

7. King, *Melville Weston Fuller*, 30.

8. Ibid., 31–35.

9. Ibid., 39–40, 63.

10. Ibid., 48–60.

11. Ibid., 64.

12. Ibid., 65.

13. Ibid., 76.

14. Ibid., 100–113.

15. Ibid., 1–7, 14.

16. Ibid., 85.

17. Ibid., 43.

18. *National Cyclopaedia of American Biography*, 33:122; King, *Melville Weston Fuller*, 11, 89, 342.

19. King, *Melville Weston Fuller*, 193–206; Carson, *Supreme Court of the United States*, 534–59.

20. King, *Melville Weston Fuller*, 165.

21. Jennings, "Bacon House," 1, 4.

22. Ibid., 4.

23. William Seale, *The Tasteful Interlude* (New York: Praeger, 1975), 109.

24. King, *Melville Weston Fuller*, 152–53.

25. Ibid., 154–62.

26. Mrs. Robert Low Bacon, personal papers.

27. King, *Melville Weston Fuller*, 152; *World Almanac*, 89.

28. King, *Melville Weston Fuller*, 328–37.

CHAPTER SIX. RENOVATION AND NEW RESIDENTS, 1911–1923

1. *Dictionary of American Biography*, 9:396–97.

2. Paul R. Baker, *Stanny: The Gilded Life of Stanford White* (New York: Free Press, 1989).

3. DACOR Bacon House Foundation, *History of the House*, 1–4.

4. Jennings, "Bacon House," 5.
5. DACOR Bacon House Foundation, *History of the House*, 1–4.
6. *National Cyclopaedia of American Biography*, 42:190–91.
7. Ibid., 28:76–77.
8. *Dictionary of American Biography*, 6:609–10.

CHAPTER SEVEN. THE BACONS HOST THE CAPITAL, 1923–1980

1. DACOR Bacon House Foundation, *History of the House*, 1–4; *Dictionary of American Biography*, 1:483–84.
2. James Brown Scott, *Robert Bacon: Life and Letters* (New York: Doubleday, 1923), 1–21, 64–65.
3. Ibid., 25–29, 105–6, 133, 171–77.
4. Ibid., 166–67.
5. Ibid., 64–65.
6. Ibid., 14–15, 287–89.
7. George F. Will, "Davis-Bacon and the Wages of Racism," *Washington Post*, February 5, 1995, sec. C, p. 7.
8. William J. Van Schreevan, comp., and Robert L. Scribner, ed., *Revolutionary Virginia: The Road to Independence, 1773–1775* (Charlottesville: University Press of Virginia, 1973), 2:3, 333, see notes 3 and 4.
9. *Dictionary of American Biography*, 3:519–20.
10. Edith Murray, ed., *Selections from the Writings of the Hon. Sir Charles Augustus Murray* (London: William Blackwood and Son, 1900), 1:4; *Burke's Peerage, Baronetage and Knightage* (London: Burke's Peerage Ltd., 1970), 873–76.
11. Donald B. Smith, *Sacred Feathers: The Reverend Peter Jones (Kahkewaquonaby) and the Mississippi Indians* (Lincoln: University of Nebraska Press, 1987), 169–70; *Concise Dictionary of American History* (New York: Scribner's Sons, 1962), 669–70, 993–95.
12. Charles Augustus Murray, *Travels in North America During the Years 1834, 1835 and 1836* (London: William Blackwood and Son, 1900), vol. 3.
13. *Debrett's Peerage and Baronetage* (London: Debrett's Peerage, 1985), 403–5.
14. Murray, *Writings of Sir Charles A. Murray*, 1:1–5.
15. *Debrett's*, 389.
16. Lyman Horace Weeks, ed., *Prominent Families of New York* (New York: Historical Company, 1897), 29; Ernest William Bowditch, "The Babcock Story" (unpublished manuscript, 1913).
17. Weeks, *Prominent Families of New York*, 29.
18. Josephine L. Murray, interview by author, September 5, 1994; August 12, 1995; and September 21, 1995.
19. Weeks, *Prominent Families of New York*, 29.
20. Forrest G. Robinson, *Love's Story Told: A Life of Henry A. Murray* (Cambridge: Harvard University Press, 1992), 8–9.
21. Josephine L. Murray, interview by author, May 7, 1996, and June 4, 1996.
22. "Virginia Murray Bacon (Mrs. Robert Low Bacon): Life Story" (unpublished manuscript prepared by Life Stories, Washington, D.C., June 1957), 1–12, among Mrs. Bacon's personal papers.
23. "Symbols of Grand Elegance," *Washington Times*, April 1, 1994, sec. C, p. 14.

24. Lawrence Kolp, secretary and curator to Virginia Bacon, 1976–80, and executive secretary, Bacon House Foundation, 1980–85, interview by author, April 12, 1996, August 9, 1996, and November 14, 1996.
25. Arthur Rubinstein, *My Many Years* (New York: Alfred A. Knopf, 1980), 555.
26. Barbara Bush, *Barbara Bush: A Memoir* (New York: Scribner's Sons, 1994), 102.
27. "Symbols of Grand Elegance," *Washington Times*, April 1, 1994, sec. C, p. 14.
28. Haupt, "Virginia Bacon, Not Ham," 91; Mrs. Robert Low Bacon, personal papers.
29. Mrs. Robert Low Bacon, personal papers.
30. Lawrence Kolp, interview by author, January 15, 1997.

CHAPTER EIGHT. TWO GREAT TRADITIONS MERGE, 1975–1986

1. Mrs. Robert Low Bacon, personal papers, 1965–75
2. DACOR Bacon House, 1964 files, National Trust for Historic Preservation.
3. Mrs. Robert Low Bacon, personal papers, 1965–75.
4. Ibid.
5. Ibid.
6. Mrs. Robert Low Bacon, personal papers, 1975–80.
7. U.S. Department of the Interior, *National Register of Historic Places* (Washington, D.C.: National Park Service, 1973).
8. Bacon House Foundation, archives, 1975–85.
9. Ibid.
10. National Trust for Historic Preservation, easement records, July 1977.
11. Mrs. Robert Low Bacon, personal papers, 1975–80.
12. Ibid.
13. Bacon House Foundation, DACOR Bacon House Foundation, archives, 1975–85.
14. Bacon House Foundation, archives, 1975–85. See pages 142–43 for details about DACOR and the merged DACOR Bacon House Foundation.
15. Ibid.
16. American Institute of Architects, archives, 1984.
17. DACOR Bacon House Foundation, general files, 1985–95.
18. Bacon House Foundation, archives, 1975–85.
19. Ibid.
20. DACOR Bacon House Foundation, general files, 1980–85.
21. Ibid.
22. *DACOR Bulletin*, May 1984.
23. Lawrence Kolp, interview by author, September 6, 1994; author's personal observations as member, DACOR board of governors 1985–91, and chairman, house committee, 1984–97.
24. *DACOR Bulletin*, May 1986 and June 1986.
25. DACOR Bacon House Foundation, general files, 1986.
26. Ibid.
27. Ibid.

CHAPTER NINE. DACOR BACON HOUSE TODAY

1. DACOR Bacon House Foundation, general files, 1995–96.
2. DACOR Bacon House Foundation, general files, 1988.

THE DACOR BACON HOUSE PORTRAITS

1. Frick Art Reference Library, New York; household inventory, 1989, general archives, DACOR Bacon House Foundation.

2. Mrs. Robert Low Bacon, personal papers, 1975–80.

3. On the back of the portrait of Elizabeth Crary appears the following note: "Elizabeth called Betsy, daughter of Joseph and Mary Denison [née Babcock] and great-great-granddaughter of George Denison and Lady [Ann] Borodell, his wife [daughter of an Irish Peer]. She [Betsy] was also the granddaughter on her mother's side of David, brother of the Hon. Joshua Babcock [Virginia Bacon's maternal great-great-great-great-grandfather]. She was born on June 19, 1780, married Peter Crary, and was the mother of Evelena, whose daughter married Samuel Denison Babcock." On the back of the portrait of Peter Crary appears this note: "Peter Crary, the 5th of that name, was descended from the King of France, beginning with Pepin LeVieux, which ancestry can be traced in *Americans of Royal Descent* by C. F. Browning. In his direct line were also the Earls of Arundel. His mother was Lucretia Palmer. He married Betsy [Elizabeth] Denison. . . . He died in 1840."

4. Mary M. Thacher, "Peter Crary's Letter from Italy—1824." In *Historical Footnotes: Bulletin of the Stonington (Conn.) Historical Society* 31, no. 4 (November 1994): 1, 7; Walter Barrett, *The Old Merchants of New York City* (New York: Worthington, 1862), 3:80–85.

5. Mrs. Robert Low Bacon, personal papers, 1975–80; DACOR Bacon House Foundation, general files, 1993–95.

6. Mrs. Robert Low Bacon, personal papers, 1975–80.

7. DACOR Bacon House Foundation, general files, 1991.

8. Morris Marples, *Wicked Uncles in Love* (London: Michael Joseph, 1972), 197–226.

9. Mrs. Robert Low Bacon, personal papers, 1940s.

10. The story that follows comes from Ernest William Bowditch, "The Babcock Story" (unpublished manuscript, 1913).

BIBLIOGRAPHY

BOOKS

Adams, Charles Francis, ed. *Memoirs of John Quincy Adams: Comprising Portions of His Diary from 1795 to 1848*. 12 vols. Philadelphia: J. B. Lippincott, 1874–77.

Babcock, Stephen, comp. *Babcock Genealogy*. New York: Easton and Mains, 1903.

Baker, Paul R. *Stanny: The Gilded Life of Stanford White*. New York: Free Press, 1989.

Barrett, Walter. *The Old Merchants of New York City*. 5 vols. New York: Worthington, 1862.

Bayley, Frank W. *The Life and Works of John Singleton Copley*. Boston: Taylor Press, 1915.

Beveridge, Albert J. *The Life of John Marshall*. 4 vols. Boston: Houghton Mifflin, 1916–19.

Birmingham, Stephen. *The Grandes Dames*. New York: Simon and Schuster, 1982.

Boorstin, Daniel Joseph. *The Americans*. 3 vols. New York: Random House, 1958–73.

Brighton, Ray A. *The Checkered Career of Tobias Lear*. Portsmouth, N.H.: Portsmouth Marine Society, 1985.

Brown, George R. *Washington: A Not Too Serious History*. Baltimore: Norman, 1930.

Bryan, Wilhelmus B. *A History of the National Capital from Its Foundation through the Period of the Adoption of the Organic Act*. 2 vols. New York: Macmillan, 1914–16.

Buchholz, Heinrich, E. *Governors of Maryland from the Revolution to the Year 1908*. Baltimore: William and Wilkins, 1908.

Bush, Barbara. *Barbara Bush: A Memoir*. New York: Scribner's Sons, 1994.

Carson, Hampton L. *The Supreme Court of the United States: Its History. Its Centennial Celebration—February 4, 1890*. Philadelphia: A. R. Keller, 1892.

Chernow, Ron. *The House of Morgan*. New York: Simon and Schuster, 1991.

Cushman, Clare, ed. *The Supreme Court Justices: Illustrated Biographies, 1789–1993*. Washington, D.C.: Congressional Quarterly, 1993.

Dumschott, Fred W. *Washington College*. Chestertown, Md.: Washington College Press, 1980.

Duvall, Elizabeth S. "The Hynson-Ringgold House of Chestertown." In *Three Centuries of American Life*. Chestertown, Md.: Kent County Historical Society, 1988.

Frary, I. T. *They Built the Capitol*. Richmond, Va.: Garrett and Massie, 1940.

Goode, James M. *Capital Losses: A Cultural History of Washington's Destroyed Buildings*. Washington, D.C.: Smithsonian Institution Press, 1979.

Gouverneur, Marion. *As I Remember: Recollections of American Society During the Nineteenth Century*. New York: Appleton, 1911.

Green, Constance McLaughlin. *A History of the Capital, 1800–1878 and 1879–1950*. 2 vols. Princeton: Princeton University Press, 1962.

Hamlin, Talbot. *Benjamin Henry Latrobe*. New York: Oxford University Press, 1955.

Hilton, Suzanne. *A Capital Capital City, 1790–1814*. New York: Atheneum Macmillan, 1992.

Kelly, C. Brian. *Best Little Stories from the White House*. With *First Ladies in Review* by Ingrid Smyer. Charlottesville, Va.: Montpelier Publishing, 1992.

King, Willard L. *Melville Weston Fuller: Chief Justice of the United States, 1888–1910*. New York: Macmillan, 1950.

Lear, Tobias. *Observations on the River Potomack, the Country Adjacent, and the City of Washington*. New York: Samuel Loudon and Son, 1793.

Marples, Morris. *Wicked Uncles in Love*. London: Michael Joseph, 1972.

McGrath, Francis Sims. *Pillars of Maryland*. Richmond, Va.: Dietz Press, 1950.

McGurn, Barrett. *America's Court: The Supreme Court and the People*. Golden, Colo.: Fulcrum, 1997.

Miller, Hope Ridings. *Great Houses of Washington, D.C.* Washington, D.C.: Clarkson N. Potter, 1969.

Moore, Derry. *Washington Homes of the Capital*. New York: Viking, 1982.

Murray, Charles Augustus. *Travels in North America During the Years 1834, 1835 and 1836*. 3 vols. London: William Blackwood and Son, 1900.

Murray, Edith, ed. *Selections from the Writings of the Hon. Sir Charles Augustus Murray*. 2 vols. London: William Blackwood and Son, 1900.

Rash, Bryson B. *Footnote Washington: Tracking the Engaging, Humorous and Surprising Bypaths of Capital History*. McLean, Va.: EPM Publications, 1983.

Reps, John W. *Washington on View: The Nation's Capital Since 1790*. Chapel Hill: University of North Carolina Press, 1991.

Robinson, Forrest G. *Love's Story Told: A Life of Henry A. Murray*. Cambridge: Harvard University Press, 1992.

Rubinstein, Arthur. *My Many Years*. New York: Alfred A. Knopf, 1980.

Scharf, John Thomas. *History of Maryland*. 3 vols. Hatboro, Pa.: Tradition Press, 1967.

Scott, James Brown. *Robert Bacon: Life and Letters*. New York: Doubleday, 1923.

Seale, William. *The Tasteful Interlude*. New York: Praeger, 1975.

Smith, Donald B. *Sacred Feathers: The Reverend Peter Jones (Kahkewaquonaby) and the Mississippi Indians*. Lincoln: University of Nebraska Press, 1987.

Van Schreevan, William J., comp., and Robert L. Scribner, ed. *Revolutionary Virginia: The Road to Independence, 1773–1775*. 2 vols. Charlottesville: University Press of Virginia, 1973.

Warren, Charles. *The Supreme Court in United States History.* 2 vols. Littleton, Colo.: Fred B. Rothman, 1897.

Weeks, Lyman Horace, ed. *Prominent Families of New York.* New York: Historical Company, 1897.

Welles, Albert. *The Babcock Family.* New York: Munsell and Rowland, 1861.

White, Frank F., Jr. *Governors of Maryland, 1777–1970.* Annapolis: Maryland Hall of Records Commission, 1970.

REFERENCE WORKS

Academic American Encyclopedia. 22 vols. Danbury, Conn.: Grolier, 1992.

Appleton's Encyclopaedia of American Biography. 7 vols. New York: D. Appleton, 1888–1901.

Biographical Cyclopedia of Representative Men of Maryland and District of Columbia. Baltimore: National Biographical Publishing Company, 1879.

Burke's Peerage, Baronetage and Knightage. London: Burke's Peerage Ltd., 1970.

Concise Dictionary of American History. New York: Scribner's Sons, 1962.

Debrett's Peerage and Baronetage. London: Debrett's Peerage, 1985.

Dictionary of American Biography. 22 vols. New York: Scribner's Sons, 1927–95.

Encyclopaedia of American History. New York: Harper and Row, 1976.

Encyclopaedia of the North American Colonies. New York: Scribner's Sons, 1993.

National Cyclopaedia of American Biography. 75 vols. New York: James T. White, 1888–1986.

Who Was Who in America, 1879–1942. Chicago: A. Marquis, 1966.

Who Was Who in America, Historic Volume, 1607–1896. Chicago: A. Marquis, 1963.

World Almanac. New York: World Almanac, 1989.

PAMPHLETS, MAGAZINE ARTICLES, BULLETINS, REPORTS, ET CETERA

Bacon, Mrs. Robert Low [Virginia Murray]. Personal papers, 1965–80. DACOR Bacon House Foundation and Georgetown University Library.

Bacon House Foundation. Archives, 1975–80.

Beard, Patricia. "Follies," *Town and Country,* April 1993.

Columbia Historical Society. Records, vol. 8, 1905.

The Congressional Directory. Washington, D.C.: U.S. Government Printing Office, 1831–32.

DACOR Bacon House Foundation. *History of the House.* Washington, D.C.: DACOR Bacon House Foundation, May 1986. Summary.

DACOR Bulletin. Various issues, 1984–86.

"The Federal Home Loan Board Building: Its Effect on the Winder Building and Related Properties." Washington, D.C.: Advisory Council on Historic Preservation, March 1974. Report.

Fuller, Robert. "Memories of Maine's Faded Famous: Melville Weston Fuller and James G. Blaine." Address before the Maine Historical Society, 1990.

Haupt, Frederick, III. "Virginia Bacon, Not Ham." *Virginia Country,* February 1987.

Jennings, J. L. Sibley. "Bacon House." J. L. Sibley Jennings, AIA, and Associates, Architects (February 1983). DACOR Bacon House Foundation. Report.

Thacher, Mary M. "Peter Crary's Letter from Italy—1824." *Historical Footnotes: Bulletin of the Stonington (Conn.) Historical Society*, 31, no. 4 (November 1994).

van Horn, Henry. "The American Portraits from the Collection of Arthur Meeker, Esq." *Town and Country*, February 21, 1921.

Wickwire, Franklin B. "Go On and Be Brave: The Battle of Point Pleasant," *Timeline* (Ohio Historical Society), August–September 1987.

INTERVIEWS

Battle, Hon. Lucius D. President, Bacon House Foundation, 1975–85; first vice president, DACOR Bacon House Foundation, 1985–87. Interviewed May 12, 1994; April 3, 1995; April 11, 1996; and November 14, 1996.

Howland, Richard H. Member, board of directors, Bacon House Foundation, 1975–85. Interviewed February 7 and 20, 1995; November 14, 1996; and August 7, 1997.

Kolp, Lawrence. Private secretary and curator to Virginia Bacon, 1972–80; executive director, Bacon House Foundation, 1980–85; and manager, DACOR Bacon House, 1985–89. Interviewed September 6, 1994; September 19, 1995; April 12, 1996; November 14, 1996; June 15, 1997; and August 5 and 12, 1997.

Murray, Josephine L. Daughter of Henry Alexander Murray Jr. and niece of Virginia Murray Bacon. Interviewed September 5, 1994; August 12, 1995; September 21, 1995; May 7, 1996; and June 4, 1996.

Stevas, Alexander L. Retired clerk of the U.S. Supreme Court. Interviewed May 12, 1994, and October 28, 1996.

NEWSPAPERS

New York Times
Washington Post
Washington Times

INDEX

Page numbers in italics refer to illustrations.

DACOR BACON HOUSE FOUNDATION

1801 F STREET, N.W.

WASHINGTON, D.C. 20006

(202) 682-0500